GENEALOGICAL DATA
FROM
CUMBERLAND COUNTY
NEW JERSEY
WILLS

Abstracted by
H. STANLEY CRAIG

Southern Historical Press, Inc.
Greenville, South Carolina

This volume was reproduced from
An 1932 edition located in the
Publisher's private Library
Greenville, South Carolina

All rights reserved. No part of this publication may be reproduced,
stored in a retrieval system, transmitted in any form, posted
on to the web in any form or by any means without
the prior written permission of the publisher.

Please direct all correspondence and orders to:

www.southernhistoricalpress.com
or
SOUTHERN HISTORICAL PRESS, Inc.
PO Box 1267
375 West Broad Street
Greenville, SC   29601
southernhistoricalpress@gmail.com

Originally published: Merchantville, NJ, 1932
Copyright 1932 by H. Stanley Craig
ISBN #0-89308-799-8
All rights Reserved.
Printed in the United States of America

PREFACTORY

Cumberland County was set off from Salem County and erected into a county by Act of the Assembly on January 19, 1747/8 The data from wills proved from that year to 1781 is taken from the Abstracts of Wills of New Jersey; from 1781 to 1804, from the original wills filed with the Secretary of State; and from 1804 to 1861, from the records of the Surrogate of Cumberland County.

For data on families residing in this locality prior to 1748, see "Salem County Genealogical Data," Vol. I.

In making searches the change in the meaning of words should be considered. In many of the early wills the words son-in-law and daughter-in-law mean stepson and stepdaughter; father-in-law means stepfather; and cousin means nephew, or neice.

GENEALOGICAL DATA FROM
CUMBERLAND COUNTY WILLS

ABRAMS

Ezekiel, Fairfield, will Dec. 23, 1827; proved Nov. 20, 1828. Wife, Margaret. Children mentioned.

ADAMS

William, Hopewell, will Jan. 15, 1790; proved Sept. 30, 1790. Children Lemuel, Philathea, Elizabeth, William and John.

ADCOCK

George, Bridgeton, will Mar. 25, 1853; proved Apr. 9, 1853. Wife, Hannah. Son, David W.

AGER

John, Deerfield, will June 28, 1859; proved Nov. 4, 1859. Wife, Matilda. Children, James, Harriet Bluy (?), Rebecca Robbins, and John.

AMBLER

John, Deerfield, will Nov. 29, 1794; proved May 16, 1796. Wife, Zeruiah. Children, John, David, Ooen, Peter, Paul, Jacob, Patience, Dorcas, Hannah and Phebe. Wife's daughter, Rachel Harris.

ANDERSON

Theodosia, Deerfield, will July 20, 1785; proved Apr. 11, 1786; Sisters, Rumolla Elmer, Victorina Bateman and Rachel Elmer.

ANDREWS

Jeremiah, Fairfield, will Oct. 17, 1821; proved Sept. 9, 1823. Sons, Josiah and Samuel. Grandchildren, Ann, Isaac, Jacob, Joseph, Andrew, Zadock and Caroline, children of son Samuel; and Edo Wick.

ARMSTRONG

George, will Apr. 21, 1797; proved June 15, 1799. No relationship shown.

ARNOLD

John, Newport, will Oct. 3, 1819; proved Dec. 2, 1819. Wife, Deborah.

AYARS

Anne, Stow Creek, June 30, 1790; proved Mar. 17, 1791. Children, Seth, Kezia Swinney, Deborah, and Anne Wood (dec'd). Grandsons, Obadiah and Adnah Wood. Sons-in-law, Vallantine Swinney and Stephen Ayars.

Caleb, Stow Creek, will Aug. 1, 1771; proved Aug. 13, 1771. Children, Jonathan, Joseph, Pacience Bonham, Isaac, Hannah Parvin, Keziah Robins, Abigail. Grandchildren, Micajah, Elijah and Azariah, sons of Nathan Ayars. Son-in-law James McFerson. Cousin, William, son of Caleb Barratt.

Elijah, Stow Creek, will Dec. 23, 1809; proved Feb. 23, 1818. Wife, Sarah. Children, Margaret Randolph, Claricy Swinney, Reese, Clayton, Oswell and Jonathan.

Jacob Randolph m. Margaret Ayars, July 28, 1800.[1]

Isaac, Stow Creek, will Aug. 15, 1771; proved Mar. 7, 1787. Children, Samuel, John, Elisha and Mark.

John, Hopewell, will Feb. 2, 1759; proved Mar. 13, 1759. Brother, Halbridge Ayars. Sisters, Sarah, Rebekah and Tabitha. Cousins, John and Abijah, sons of Benjamin Ayars; Hambilton

---

[1]County Clefk's records.

and Rachel, children of Aaron Ayars; and Thomas, son of Joseph Bivins.

Jonathan, Stow Creek, will Apr. 9, 1775; proved Sept. 26, 1782. Wife, Pheby. Children, Caleb, Jonathan, Zerviah, Sarah, Pheby, Dorcus, Unis and Rachel.

Joshua, Fairfield, will May 2, 1759; proved May 24, 1759. Wife, Anne. Children, Seth, Philipp, Esther Davis, Hezekiah, Deborah, and an expected child.

Nathan, Stow Creek, will Nov. —, 1762; proved Mar. 13, 1769. Wife, Elizabeth. Children, Nathan, Micajah, Elijah and Azariah.

Noah, Bridgeton, will Sept. 11, 1851; proved March 9, 1853. Children, Elizabeth wife of Robert Hood, Samuel L., Joseph S., John H., Addi, Thomas J., James, and Sally Randolph. Grandson, Noah. son of Joseph S. Ayars.
Robert Hood m. Elizabeth Ayres, Feb. 2, 1842.[1]

Parthenia, Hopewell, will Sept. 28, 1830; proved Oct. 30, 1833. Children, Caleb S. Hall, Hannah Ayars, Elizabeth Davis, Levi B. Hall and Aaron S. Hall.

Philip, Jr., July 31, 1789; proved Dec. 31, 1789. Wife mentioned, but not by name. Children, Philip and Lidya. Son-in-law, Job Ayars.

Rebekah, Stow Creek, widow of Caleb, will Dec. 14, 1766; proved Oct. 31, 1774. Children, Sarah Bivins, Tabitha Francis, and Stephen. Son-in-law, Joseph Bivins.

Sarah (wid.), Hopewell, Aug. 10, 1812; Proved Mar. 28, 1825. No relationship shown.

Sarah, Stow Creek, will Jan. 1, 1830; proved Aug. 1, 1831. Children, Susan B. Bonham and Rebecca M. Bacon.

AYERS

Asa, will March 9, 1846; proved Nov. 1, 1858. Wife, Hannah. Daughter, Jane Eliza wife of Isaac S. F. Randolph.
Isaac S. F. Randolph m. Jane Eliza Ayars, May 1, 1842.[1]

---

[1]County Clerk's records.

Aulay, Stoe Creek, will Mar. 4, 1853; proved Mar. 30, 1853. Children, Artelia wife of Samuel J. Ayres, and Tamar wife of Richard B. Davis. Artelia, dau. of Richard and Tamar Davis; Phebe Malvina and Samuel J., chd. of Samuel and Artelia Ayres. Nephew, Belford E. Davis.

Richard B. Davis m. Tamar Ayars, Nov. 21, 1840.[1]

Caleb, Hopewell, will May 27, 1759; proved Feb. 5, 1760. Wife, Rebeca. Children, Stephen, Halbridge, William, Sarah, Rebekah, Tabitha and Benjamin.

Phebe, Stoe Creek, will Aug. 18, 1848; proved Feb. 10, 1852. Brother, Thomas. Nephew, Abel Davis.

Reece, Hopewell, will Feb. 28, 1855; proved Feb. 26, 1858. Brother, Clayton Ayres.

Zara, Stoe Creek, will July 27, 1847; proved Feb. 8, 1848. Wife, Maria. Children, Eli, Almedia and Albert.

BACON

Aaron, will Jan. 21, 1789; proved Dec. 26, 1800. Wife, Hannah. Children Joseph and Pheby.

Amos, Stow Creek, will Feb. 19, 1780; proved Apr. 1, 1780. Wife, Anna. Children, Amos, Priscilla, Denn and Daniel.

Charles, Greenwich, will Oct. 3, 1791; proved Dec. 22, 1812. Children, Thomas, Benjamin, David, and Rachel Sheppard.

Daniel, Greenwich, will June 14, 1813; proved Aug. 31, 1813. Wife, Hannah. Children, Ephraim, Daniel, John S., Tabitha and Hannah.

Edmund, Greenwich, Feb. 15, 1778; proved Sept. 27, 1790. Wife, Mary. Children, Joseph, and an expected child. Brothers, Joseph, Jesse and Richard Bacon. Aunt, Elizabeth Randolph.

Edmund Bacon m. Mary Eldridge, Mar. 28, 1766.[2]

Enos, Hopewell, will June 11, 1797; proved July 24, 1897. Wife, Hannah. Children, Enos, Samuel, Joseph, Sarah Husted, Rachel

---

[1] County Clerk's records.
[2] New Jersey Marriage Licenses.

FROM CUMBERLAND COUNTY WILLS

Rankin, Mary and Richard. Son-in-law, David Husted. Brother-in-law, Sheppard Bacon.

George, will Aug. 8, 1849; proved Feb. 5, 1857. Wife, Naomi. Children, Margaret, Richard W., Francis, Mary W., and George (decd.). Grandchildren, James and George Withers and Eliza A., Mary and George R., children of son George.

Isaac, Hopewell, will Nov. 22, 1775; proved Jan. 1776; Wife, Mary. Children, Philah, Hannah, Mary and Anna.
Isaac Bacon m. Mary Sayre, Feb. 29, 1764.[1]

Isaac, Greenwich, will Feb. 1, 1763; proved March 25, 1763. Wife, Sarah. Son, Abel. Nephew, John Shephard. Brother, Obediah Robbins.

Jacob, Greenwich, will Nov. 13 1784; proved Mar. 19, 1785. Sisters, Anna Ware, and Rachel wife of Obadiah Robins. Nephew, Daniel Shepherd.

James, Greenwich, will Mar. 1, 1775; proved Mar. 27, 1775. Wife, Sarah. Children, David, Isaac, Rachel and Abigail.

Jeremiah, Stow Creek, will Jan. 16, 1768; proved Feb. 12, 1768. Wife, Rachel. Children, Shepherd, Sarah, Elizabeth, Hannah and Liddea. Brother-in-law, John Ewing.

Job, Greenwich, will Aug. 1, 1813; proved June 20, 1814. Wife, Ruth. Children, John, Job, Martha Reeve, Mary, Sarah S., Ann T., Josiah and Morris. Brother, George Bacon.

John, Greenwich, will April 18, 1781; proved July 23, 1791. Wife Mary. Children, John, George, Ann, Elizabeth, Job.

Joseph, Hopewell, will Aug. 11, 1818; proved Aug. 28, 1818. Wife, Phebe. Half-brother, John Harris.

Lot, Greenwich, will Dec. 5, 1811; proved Jan. 8, 1812. Wife, Barbary. Children, Jeremiah, Isaac, John, Mary Miller and Rebecca. Brother, Mark Bacon.

Margaret, Greenwich, will Jan. 21, 1769; proved May 21, 1769. Children, Joseph, Richard, Jesse, Deborah, Esther, Margaret,

---

[1] New Jersey Marriage Licenses.

Prudence and Elizabeth.

Mary, Greenwich, will Jan. 17, 1764; proved Apr. 20, 1764. Children, Nathan, Rachel Robbins, Anne Ware and Jacob. Granddaughter, Mary Sayres.

Mary, Greenwich, will Apr. 17, 1848; proved Nov. 13, 1854. Children, Edward S., Abel D., Isabella J., Kezziah Ann and Rebecca T.

Mary H., Greenwich, will Apr. 11, 1856; proved Sept. 15, 1860. Children, Lewis N., William S., Jane wife of Aaron Clements, Phebe wife of Samuel Watson, and Sarah wife of B. Franklin Maul.
Aaron Clements m. Jane P. Bacon, Jan. 29, 1840.[1]
Samuel Watson m. Phebe M. Bacon, Dec. 7, 1853.[1]
Benjamin F. Maul m. Sarah, B. Bacon, Dec 13, 1848.[1]

Sarah (wid. of Uriah), Stoe Creek, will Apr. 5, 1839; proved Nov. 16, 1843. Sisters, Elizabeth Noble and Hannah Ayars. Brothers, Zebediah and William. Nephews and neices, Robert Dayton Davis; Louis, Ann, Hannah, Rebecca, Lydia, Jane; Hannah wife of Nathan D. Ayres; Isaac N. Davis.

Sarah S., Hopewell, Nov. 24, 1837; proved Sept. 13, 1842. Sister, Elizabeth Harris. Half-sister, Rachel wife of Enos Bacon. Nephew, Alva Harris.
Enos Bacon m. Rachel Harris, Oct. 4, 1796.[1]

Susannah, Stoe Creek, will Sept. 21, 1806; proved June 20, 1809. Children, Hannah, Mary and Peniah.

Thomas, Greenwich, will July 17, 1771; proved Feb. 8, 1772. Wife, Ellenor. Children, Rachel, Dorcas, Ruth, Ellenor, John and Charles. Brother John Bacon.

Thomas, will June 17, 1813; proved Nov. 6, 1813. Children, Elizabeth, Thomas and Ebenezer.

Uriah, Roadstown, will Apr. 9, 1828; proved Feb. 11, 1831. Daughter, Elizabeth Davis. Grandson, Joseph Bacon.

William, Bacons Neck, June 11, 1782; proved Nov. 11, 1782.

---

[1]County Clerk's records.

Wife, Tabitha. Children, Daniel, Abel, William, Phebe Ludlam, Sarah and Grace.
Norton Ludlam m. Phebe Bacon, Nov. 8, 1779.[1]

William, Bacons Neck, will May 13, 1838; proved Aug. 29, 1838. Wife, Mary. Children, Lewis H., William, Mary Probasco, Jane, Phebe, Margerite and Sarah. Son-in-law, John Probasco.
John Probasco m. Mary Bacon, Nov. 13, 1833.[2]

BAILY

Bagwell, Downe, will Jan. 27, 1846; proved Apr. 12, 1848. Wife, Jane. Children, James, Rachel wife of John Rose, Edward, Daniel, John, Bagwell, and Nancy wife of Amariah Robinson. Son-in-law, James Parsons.
John Rose m. Rachel Bailey, July 7 1825.[2]
Amariah Robinson m. Nancy Bailey, Jan. 30, 1836.[2]
James Parsons m. Susan Bailey, Oct. 9, 1814.[2]

Daniel, Downe, will June 9, 1856; proved June 30, 1858. Wife, Elizabeth. Son, Joseph.

BARKER

Richard, Stow Creek, will Jan. 24, 1765; proved Feb. 19, 1765. Wife, Ruth. Children, John, Samuel, William, Isaac, Mary and Richard.

BARNES

Samuel, Fairfield, will Feb. 25, 1757; proved Jan. 30, 1858. Children, Jonathan, Abraham and John. Grandson Thomas Barnes.

BARNS

Jonathan, Cohansey, will Aug. 23, 1777; proved Sept. 19, 1777. Daughter. Damaress. Brother-in-law, John Barnes.

BARRACLIFF

John, will Apr. 9, 1790; proved Oct. 12, 1790. Children, Ruth Shints, and George.

---

[1] New Jersey Marriage Licenses.
[2] County Clerk's records.

BARRATT

Caleb, Hopewell, will Aug. 19, 1757; proved Jan. 12, 1758. Wife, Abigail. Children, Caleb, Joshua, James, Elizabeth Mulford, Hannah Hall, Abigail Shepard, Rebekah and Sarah.

Abel Sheppard m. Abigail Barratt, 1754.[1]

Caleb, Hopewell, will Jan. 4, 1796; proved June 16, 1797. Wife, Sarah. Wife's brother, Reuben son of Jonathan Jarman. Nephews Caleb son of James Barratt, and Jonathan son of John Jarman.

James, Hopewell, will Feb. 3, 1781; proved Mar. 6, 1781. Wife, Sarah. Children, Caleb, Elizabeth, Sarah, Abigail, Deborah, James and Thomas. Grandchildren, Sarah daughter of Thomas, and Sarah daughter of James.

BARRETT

Joshua, Hopewell, will Nov. 15, 1795; proved Dec. 28, 1795. Sons, Joshua and Caleb.

William, Downe, will Sept. 3, 1793; proved Oct. 22, 1793. Wife, Mary. Children, Lettisha and William. Grandson, Leonard Shaw.

BARROW

Peter, will May 24, 1859; proved Nov. 11, 1859. Daughter, Emeline Hasen. Granddaughter, Emily daughter of Emeline.

BATEMAN

Aaron, Fairfield, will Jan. 11, 1779; proved Jan. 21, 1779. Wife, Elizabeth. Sons, John and Aaron. Daughters mentioned, but not by name. An expected child.

Abigail, Fairfield, will Nov. 26, 1802; proved June 7, 1804. Children, Abigail Ray, Elener Dixon, James Ray and Joseph Bateman.

Burgin, Fairfield, will Aug. 17, 1793; proved Oct. 23, 1793. Wife, Susanna. Children, Ephraim and Burgin; others mentioned, but not by name.

---

[1] Miscellaneous Biographies.

Daniel, Fairfield, will Apr. 10, 1776; proved Mar. 12, 1777. Wife, Abigail. Children, Ruhamah, Sarah, Abigail, Nathan, William, Joseph, Reuben, Jonathan, Burgan and Daniel.

David, Fairfield, will Dec. 13, 1844; proved June 23, 1846. Children, George (decd.), David, Esli, Israel, Annah, Precilla, Charles (decd.), Anna, Margaret. Grandsons, George and Esli, sons of George.

Elkanah, Fairfield, will July 31, 1833; proved Aug. 14, 1833. Wife Sabrina. Sons, Elkanah and Aaron.

Ephraim, Cedarville, will Nov. 27, 1827; proved Feb. 11, 1829. Wife mentioned, but not by name. Children, Benjamin, Lydia, William, Eleazar and Harriet. Brothlr, Burgin.

Harvey, Fairfield, will Aug. 10, 1850; proved Nov. 30, 1850. Wife, Jane E. Children, Mary, Joseph, Lemuel, Jane E. D., and Martha. Brother, Jasper. Son-in-law, Ephraim Bateman.

Job, Fairfield, will Dec. 24, 1759; proved Jan. 21, 1760. Wife, Martha. Son, Aaron.

John, Sr., Fairfield, will May 21, 1785; proved Sept. 23, 1786. Wife, Jude. Children, Isaac, Sarah Robinson, Priscilla Asstins, and Hellen James. Grandson, Thomas Bateman.

John Bateman m. Judith Hand, July 27, 1771.[1]

John, Fairfield, will July 26, 1813; proved Nov. 29, 1813 Children, Thomas, Lodemy Burt, and Polly.

Jonathan, Fairfield, will Dec. 24, 1822; proved Mar. 25, 1823. Wife mentioned, but not by name. Grandchildren, Leonard, Abigail S., and Julia Ann Bateman.

Joseph, will Sept. 19, 1784; proved Dec. 19, 1785. Children, Joseph, Jane, Elizabeth wife of Isaac Bennet, and Dorcas wife of James Bennet.

Joseph, Fairfield, will Apr. 5. 1831; proved May 23, 1832. Wife, Polly. Children, Joseph, Polly Newcomb, Elizabeth Newcomb, Lodemy Fithian, Harvey and Jasper. Grandchildren, Casper Gregory, Andrew Jackson, Mary Ann and Elias, children of son Joseph.

---

[1] New Jersey Marriage Licenses.

Moses, Fairfield, will June 28, 1841; proved Aug. 25, 1841. Children, Eli E., Elkanah (decd), Adrian, Amos and Nathaniel. Grandchildren, Elkanah and Aaron sons of Elkanah; and Hannah Bateman. Daughters-in-law, Lovisa and Sabra.

Moses, Jr., Downs, will not dated; proved Dec. 1, 1854. Brother, Elkanah.

Nathan, Deerfield, will May 15, 1759; proved Aug. 28, 1759. Wife Abigail. Son, Manoah. Son-in-law, Dan Robinson.

Peter, Deerfield, will May 8, 1759; proved June 16, 1759. Wife, Elizabeth. Children, Nathan, Peter, Moses, Hannah Gentry, Nemiah and William.

Reuben, will May 19, 1849; proved June 2, 1849. Wife, Mary. Children, Eli D., Matilda Thompson, Charlotte, Reuben, Theophilus and Elmer O. Grandchild, Ella L. Bateman.

Rhoda, Cedarville, will Feb. 6, 1838; proved Feb. 11, 1853. Children, Rebecca wife of Henry Powell, Lydia and Rhoda Bateman.

Thomas, Cohansey, will Jan. 31, 1759; proved Mar. 10, 1759. Wife, Mary. Children, Rebecca and Phebe; five others mentioned, but not by name.

Timothy, Fairfield, will Feb. 12, 1761; proved July 12, 1779. Wife, Rebecca. Children, Amos, Eli, Mary and Freelove.

William, will Aug. 17, 1829; proved Jan. 23, 1836. Wife, Abigail. Children, John, Esther wife of William Smith, and Sarah. Grandsons, William A. Smith and William Bateman. Wife's son, Nathaniel Howell.

BEDENT

John, Fairfield, will June 28, 1758; proved Aug. 18, 1761. Wife, Abigail. Children, Elizabeth Hildridge, Mary Robbins, Rebeka Blizard, Naomi Blizard and Keziah Dean. Grandsons, Moses Barratt and Samuel Shepherd.

BELL

Robert, Maurice River, will July 25, 1824; proved Apr. 18, 1831. Wife, Elizabeth. Daughter, Sarah T. Lowery. Grandchildren, Elizabeth, Ann Maria, Mary G., and John T. Lowery.

BENNETT

Jeremiah, Bridgeton, will June 3, 1810; proved June 26, 1810. Wife, Joanna. Children, Ruth S. Elmer, Jeremiah, Samuel and Jane.

Timothy Elmer m. Ruth Bennett, Nov. 30, 1807.[1]

Samuel, Fairfield, will Oct. 21, 1772; proved Oct. 4, 1789. Sons, Obadiah, Samuel, Nathan and Jonathan. Daughters mentioned, but not by name.

BERRIMAN

Thomas, Cohansey, will Mar. 7, 1746/7; proved June 14, 1749. Wife Martha, Children, Annabel Johnson, Rachel Benet, Perthenia Reeves, Elizabeth, Zurviah, Hannah and John.

BERTHDEL

Christopher F. Fight, Morris River, will Oct. 13, 1823; proved Apr. 6, 1824. Wife Mary. Daughter, Catharine Sharp. Grandchildren, Sarah Fight, Elijah and Sarah Collwell.

BIAS

James, Hopewell, will May 24, 1845; proved Oct. 29, 1845. Wife, Anna.

BIGGS

William, will Jan. 2, 1794; proved Jan. 6, 1794. Wife, Rachel. Brothers, Daniel, Jeremiah and John. Nephew and neice, William son of John, and Hannah McGrange.

BISHOP

Alexander, Hopewell, will not dated; proved Mar. 4, 1817. Wife, Patience. Brother Stratton Bishop. Sister's son, John Dorton.

Daniel, Hopewell, will Jan. 29, 1771; proved Mar. 2, 1771. Wife, Rhoda. Children, Daniel; others mentioned, but not by name.

---

[1]County Clerk's records.

David, Hopewell, will June 6, 1789; proved Sept. 9, 1791. Brothers, Stratton and Alexander Bishop. Sisters, Sarah Bishop, Mary Royall and Elizabeth Dorton.

David Royall m. Mary Bishop, Dec. 31, 1788.[1]

Elizabeth (wid. of John Bishop), Hopewell, will May 4, 1784; proved June 18, 1784. Children, Straton, David, Alexander, John, Elizabeth Daten, Sarah and Mary.

Ephraim, will Dec. 3, 1840; proved Aug. 6, 1846. Wife Lydia. Children, Ephraim, Daniel, Hannah Potter, Lydia Cory, Louisa Tomlinson, Preston, Gideon K., and Martha. Grandson, Robert K. Bishop. Son-in-law, Nathan Tomlinson.

Henry Potter m. Hannah Bishop, Nov. 12, 1811.[2]
John Corey m. Lydia Bishop, Dec. 28, 1814.[2]
Nathan Tomlinson m. Louisa Bishop, Mar. 10, 1824.[3]

Ichabod, Fairfield, will Feb. 15, 1812; proved Apr. 18, 1812. Wife, Elizabeth. Children, Mary Shaw, Elizabeth, Abigail, Preston and Mertillo.

Moses, Hopewell will, June 12, 1749; proved July 8, 1749, Children, Moses, Levi, Esther, Mary, Rachel and Eunice.

Nathaniel, Cohansey, will Mar. 6, 1748/9; proved Apr. 1, 1749. Wife, Mary. Children, Isaac, Preston, Jeremiah, Zephaniah, Nathaniel, Mary Lupton, Abigail, Elizabeth and Hannah.

Stratton, Bridgeton, will not dated; proved Mar. 25, 1823. Wife, Lydia. Children, Reuben, John, Lorana wife of Hosea Nichols, and Ruth wife of Samuel Souder.

BITTER

Henry, Hopewell, will May 17, 1832; proved June 25, 1832. Wife, Phebe. Children, Daniel, Sarah Irelan, William, Henry, Zachariah, Jacob, Margaret Garton, and Elizabeth.

---

[1] Greenwich Presbyterian Church records.
[2] Records of First Presbyterian Church, Bridgeton.
[3] County Clerk's records.

BIVINS

Joseph, will Oct. 20, 1794; proved Oct. 23, 1794. Wife, Sarah. Children, David, Benjamin, Thomas, Sarah Woodrough, Rebecca Bennet, and Eunis. Grandson, Joseph son of Thomas.

BLEW

Elizabeth, Fairfield, will ———, 1779; proved Sept. 30, 1790. Children, John, and Elener Hewit.

Elizabeth, Fairfield, will Mar. 27, 1826; proved May 31, 1827. Children, Abigail Vandusin, Ruth Quixel and Elizabeth Ward.

BLISZARD

Benjamin, Fairfield, will Feb. 17, 1769; proved Feb. 26, 1771. Children, John, James, Thomas, Levi, Pheby and Ann.

Jonathan, Downe, will Aug. 14, 1803; proved Sept. 22, 1803. Wife, Rachel. An expected child. Sister, Susannah Shull, who has children, Jonathan and Rachel Shull.

BLIZARD

Jeremiah, Downe, will Feb. 18, 1824; proved Mar. 5, 1824. Children, Samuel, William, Virgil, Mason, Elizabeth wife of Benjamin Biggs, Bruceacks (?), and Philey wife of Joseph Campbell. Grandchildren, July Ann, Virgil and Pheby, children of Mason and Abigail Blizard.

Mason Blizard m. Abigail Ackley, Mar. 13, 1814.[1]

Levi, Downe, will Mar. 13, 1777; proved June 17, 1777. Wife, Theodosha. Daughter, Reuhamy. Nephew and neice, Ziba and Irana, children of brother James Blizard.

Thomas, Downe, will Jan. 27, 1835; proved June 7, 1836. Children, Daniel, Mary wife of Abraham Vanderford, Hester wife of Joseph Hickman, and Samuel.

Abraham Vandeford m. Mary Blizzard, Apr. 11, 1898.[1]

---

[1]County Clerk's records.

GENEALOGICAL DATA

BLOOMFIELD

Phebe (wid. of Moses, late of Woodbridge, N. J.), will Mar. 14 1810; proved Oct. 3, 1820. Mother, Anna Holmes (decd.). Children, Hannah wife of James Giles. Grandchildren, Maria McIlvaine, wife of Abraham Inskeep, Fannie Holmes Giles, Nancy Bloomfield Giles, daughters of James and Hannah Giles. Nephews and neices, Sarah wife of Jeremiab Buck; Jonathan, John and Ephriam sons of brother Abijah Holmes; Abijah, son of nephew Jonathan Holmes; Jackson Brewster and Mary Dare, children of Eunice Brewster; Daniel Clark, Mary wife of Ebenezer Seeley; Phebe wife of Dr. Azel Pierson, children of sister Anna Clark; and Josiah son of sister Rachel Fithian.

Ebenezer Seeley m. Mary Clark, Mar. 30, 1783.[1]
Azel Pierson m. Phebe Clark, Oct. 3, 1820.[2]

BODLEY

Elizabeth, Port Elizabeth, will June 13. 1811; proved Jan. 9, 1816. Children, Elizabeth wife of Jonathan Dollass, Joel Clark and Mary Tuft.

BONHAM

Hezekiah, Stow Creek, will Aug. 18, 1809; proved Dec. 20, 1809. Wife, Sarah. Brother, Ephraim Bonham.

Nathan, Stoe Creek, will Aug. 25, 1835; proved Nov. 29, 1836. Children, Ruel, Anna Mariah, Belford M., and Jehu. Grandchildren, Edmund M., Edgar and Martha I. Bonham.

BOON

Enoch, Hopewell, will July 11, 1830; proved Aug. 23, 1830. Children William B., Ann Hughes and Richard M.

BOOTH

Isabel, Stow Creek, will Nov. 5, 1770; proved Nov. 24, 1770. No relationship shown.

James, Hopewell, will Jan. 24, 1748/9; proved Feb. 2, 1748/9.

---

[1]New Jersey Marriage Licenses.
[2]Pierson Bible record.

FROM CUMBERLAND COUNTY WILLS

Sisters, Isabel Booth, Agnes McClong, Esther McMungall, Margaret Wood and Elizabeth Nealy. Cousin, John, son of Joseph Nealy.

BORDEN

Thomas, will June 25, 1813; proved Nov. 5, 1813. Wife, Phebe. Children, William, Thomas, Ann, and an expected child. Granddaughter, Mary, daughter of William.

BOWEN

Bacon, Stoe Creek, will Oct. 14, 1838; proved Sept. 30, 1839. Children, Zilla Ayres (dec'd), John, Esther wife of Levi Hall, and Zadock (dec'd). Grandchildren, Phineas and Amy children of Zadock.
Levi Hall m. Esther Bowen, Mar. 29, 1821.[1]

Dan, Deerfield, will proved 1790. Children, Mark, Dan, Abraham, Ephraim, Ruhamey Moore, Mary Nickol, Rebecka Smith. Grandchildren, Hosea, Eli, Ellis and Rebecka Robinson. Son-in-law, Abraham Robinson.
Elijah Moore m. Ruhama Bowen, May 27, 1783.[2]

David, Hopewell, will Jan. 1, 1808; proved Sept. 6, 1808. Wife, Ruth. Nephews and neices, Mason Smith and his wife, Jane; David, son of David and Jane Bowen; Mary, wife of Capt. George Johnston; Harriet, daughter of David and Jane Bowen; Mary, widow of David Westcott; Rachel, wife of Joseph Stockton; Mary Roberts, Nancy Stratton, Sarah, wife of Abial Jones, and Prudence, wife of James Murphew.

Enoch, Fairfield, will May 1, 1776; proved May 21, 1776. Children, Mason, Jerial, Mary, Noah, Levi, Sarah Helton, Henry, Eve Terry, Enoch, and Rachel Whitecar. Grandchildren, Garrison, Henry and Ruth, children of Jerial Bowen, and Jerushe, daughter of Sarah Helton.

---

[1] County Clerk's records.
[2] Pittsgrove Baptist Church records.

Isaac, Fairfield, will 1748; proved Sept. 2, 1748. Wife, Phebe. Children, Clephon, Isaac, Phebe, Esther and Susannah.

John, will Sept. 9, 1784; proved Jan. 22, 1785. Wife, Ann. Children, John, Constant, Mark, Lucy Hogben, Katherine Reves, Rachel Couch and Dan.

John, Downe, will Mar. 19, 1858; proved Oct. 27, 1858. Wife, Nancy. Children mentioned, but not by name.

Jonathan, Bridgeton, will Feb. 21, 1804; proved Sept. 24, 1804. Wife, Sarah. Children, Sarah Bacon, Daniel, Smith, and Rebecca Bacon. Grandchildren, Ephraim sons of Sarah Bacon; Daniel, Jesse H. and Jane, children of Smith Bowen; and Delzel, William, and Rebecca, children of Rebecca Bacon; and Mary Bowen. Neice, Mary Roberts.

Joseph, will Jan. 22, 1797; proved Mar. 25, 1803. Wife, Mary. Children, Bacon, Abigail wife of David Randall, and Joseph,
Joseph Bowen m. Mary Bacon, Dec. 22, 1761.[1]

Mark, Deerfield, will Aug. 25, 1832; proved Oct. 22, 1832. Wife, Clarissa,. Children, Mary High, Rachel Loper, Jonathan, Samuel, David, Daniel, Abraham, and Sarah.

Mnason, Fairfield, will June 9, 1826; proved Aug. 4, 1826. Wife, Hannah. Children, Daniel S., Melite, Ruth S., Mary N., Dayton J., Lemuel, Mnason and Reuben N. Granddaughter, Mary D. Bowen.

Peleg, Hopewell, will Feb. 5, 1779; proved Feb. 17, 1779. Brother, Elisha Swinney. Cousins, Amey Shepherd, Martha and Samuel Sockwell.

Phebe (formerly Phebe Parsons, wife of James Bowen), Downe, will June 25, 1853; proved Nov. 14, 1853. Children, Jehu and James Bowen, Lydia Cummins, Mary Blizzard, Margaret Hand, Hannah Biggs, Elizabeth Webb and Susan Appleton.
Thomas Biggs m. Hannah Bowing, Feb. 15, 1840.[2]

Ruth (wid. of Dan), will Feb. 4, 1818; proved Apr. 25, 1826.

---

[1] New Jersey Marriage Licenses.
[2] County Clerk's records.

Daughter, Hannah B. McLain. Stepdaughter Elizabeth wife of Robert McLain.

Ruth, Hopewell (wife of David), will Nov. 12, 1844; proved Dec. 29, 1846. Sister, Mary Brick. Nephew and neices, Dr. Enoch Fithian, Phebe Moore, Rachel Whitaker and Mary Woodruff.

Samuel, Stow Creek, will Dec. 12, 1788; proved Jan. 14, 1789. Wife, Rebeckah. Children, Samuel, Mary Loper and Rebeckah. Granddaughter, Lydia Bowen.

Seth, will Oct. 4, 1773; proved Feb. 24, 1785. Wife, Charity. Children, Seth, Temperance Matthews, Jeremiah, Landal and George. Grandchildren, Henry and Rebeckah Wescoat.
Seth Bowen m. Charity Billins, May 27, 1773.[1]

Seth, Hopewell, will Jan. 11, 1804; proved Dec. 7. 1807 "Sisters in the church," Ruth Bowen, Elizabeth Robinson, Rachel Reed and Anay Perrey.

Smith, Bridgeton, will Feb. 6, 1840; proved Feb. 26, 1840. Children, Mary widow of William Bacon; Jane wife of John Buck, Dr. William S., Jesse H. and Smith. Daughter-in-law, Sarah wife of Jesse. Grandson, Smith Bowen.
John Buck m. Jane Bowen, May 5, 1819.[2]

William, Bridgeton, will May 5, 1824; proved Jan. 17, 1824. Wife, Martha. Children, Nellie, Betsey, Sally, Polly, William and John.

BOWER

Ebenezer, Fairfield, will June 13, 1767; proved Feb. 28, 1769. Wife, Priscilla. Children, John, Hannah Preston and David.
Ebenezer Bower m. Priscilla Burrows, May 1, 1730.[1]

John, will Sept. 14, 1801; proved Sept. 18, 1801. Wife, Nancy.

Priscilla, Fairfield, will Sept. 17, 1769; proved Nov. 27, 1769. Children, David, John, and Hannah Preston. Grandchildren, Burrhus and Lucy Brooks.

---

[1]New Jersey Marriage Licenses.
[2]County Clerk's records.

BOYD

Amy, Deerfield, will Mar. 26, 1777; proved May 6, 1777. Children, James and Sarah.

Mary, Bridgeton, will Aug. 7, 1801; proved Mar. 13, 1813. Children, Hannah Potter, Sarah and James. Grandsons, James B. and Robert B. Potter.

William, Deerfield, will Aug. 19, 1774; proved Sept. 7, 1774. Children, James and Sarah.

BRADFORD

Henry, Downe, will Nov. 26, 1859; proved Jan. 14, 1861. Wife, Sarah. Children, Enos, Sarah, Rhoda, Elizabeth, Laressa, James, David (dec'd), Sinai and Phebe. Grandchildren, Samuel and Henry, sons of David. David's wife has a daughter, Nancy.

David Bradford m. Mary Bateman, Oct. 2, 1836.[1]

Silas, Downe, will Apr. 17, 1813; proved May 19, 1813. Wife, Mary. Sons, Enos, Elias and Henry.

Silas Bradford m. Mary Williams, July 25, 1804.[1]

William, Cohansey, will Sept. 11, 1747; proved Mar. 25, 1749. Wife, Mary. Sons Reymond and William. Son-in-law, Benjamin Parvin.

BRADWAY

Abigail, Fairfield, will Apr. 3, 1759; proved April 16, 1759. Children, Jeremiah Harris, Abigail Harris and Reuben Harris.

Adna, Stoe Creek, will Feb. 2 1860; proved June 19, 1860. Wife, Lydia. Children, Edward, Elisha, Adna, Jacob and Jonathan. Grandchildren, Andrew G., Frank, Edgar, Mary M. and Nathan Adna Bradway.

BRAGG

John, Fairfield, will Nov. 4, 1767; proved Apr. 17, 1772. Wife, Mary. Children, Henry, John, Ann, Mary and Phineas.

---

[1]County Clerk's records.

BRANHAM

Susannah, will Feb. 26, 1849; proved May 12, 1849. Sister Cecelia Kenamon.

BREWSTER

Francis, Greenwich, will Nov. 16, 1768; proved Dec. 2, 1768. Wife, Rebecca. Children, Gilbert, Joseph, Samuel, Hannah, Ruth, Anne, Ebenezer, Benjamin and Daniel.
Francis Brewster m. Rebecca Peck, Jan. 6, 1758.[1]

Francis G., Bridgeton, will July 12, 1856; proved Oct. 25, 1856. Wife, Ruth T. Children, Mary and Edwin.

BRICK

John, Cohansey, will Aug. 29, 1737; proved Apr. 26, 1753. Wife, Hannah. Children, William, Elizabeth Dunlap; Hannah Hancock, Joshua, Joseph and John. Grandsons, John and Ephriam Worthington.

John, Hopewell, Dec. 6, 1757; proved Mar 1, 1758. Wife, Ann. Children, John, Joseph, Mary Hall, Elizabeth Reeve, Ann, Hannah, Ruth and Jane.

Joseph, Stow Creek, will Mar. 29, 1763; proved Apr. 27, 1763. Wife, Elizabeth. Children, William, Ephraim, Elizabeth, Hannah, John, Rachel and Joseph.

Joshua, Port Elizabeth, will Sept. 21, 1857; proved June 6, 1860. Children, Hannah Willets, Caroline Bickley and Joshua. Grandchildren, Horace P. Bickley, John Howard Willets, and George son of Joshua Brick, Jr.

Mary, Hopewell, will Oct. 26, 1793; proved Dec. 30, 1794. Sisters, Rachel Clark, Ruth Fithian, Hannah Leake and Amy Moore. Brother, Joel Fithian.

William, will Oct. 30, 1766; proved Oct. 12, 1767. Brothers, Ephraim and John. Sister, Rachel. Father-in-law, Jacob Brown.

---

[1] New Jersey Marriage Licenses.

BRIGHT

Elizabeth, Hopewell, will 1854; proved Jan. 24, 1859 Children, John and Charles Bright.

Jesse, Hopewell, will Feb. 22, 1835; proved Apr. 11, 1842. Children, John and Charles.

Michael, Downe, will Aug. 6, 1779; proved Nov. 11, 1780. Brother-in-law, Jonadab Shepherd.

William, Downe, will July 23, 1786; proved Jan. 8, 1787. Wife, Elizabeth. Children, Anna, William and Levi.

BRITHOLD

Philip, Maurice River, will Apr. 4, 1816; proved May 14, 1816. Wife, Elizabeth. Children, John, Margaret and Elizabeth.

BROADWATER

Thomas E., Bridgeton, will Aug. 11, 1852; proved Oct. 11, 1854. Uncle, Thomas Broadwater.

BROOKS

Almarine, Bridgeton, will Sept. 26, 1823; proved Feb. 10, 1824. Wife, Sarah. Children, Catharine Streeper and Phebe Paul.
Christopher Streeper m. Catharine Brooks. Dec. 7, 1822.[1]
Hiram Paul m. Phebe Brooks, Jan. 20, 1823.[2]

Henry, Deerfield, will Feb. 18, 1749/50; proved Mar. 5, 1749/50. Children, Mahattable, Henry, Lydia and Joel. Brother, Josiah Brooks.

John, Hopewell, will Jan. 6, 1797; proved Apr. 2, 1799. Wife, Mary. Daughter, Rachel.
John Brooks m. Mary Jenkins, Dec. 15, 1778.[3]

Sarah (widow of Almarine), Bridgeton, will Oct. 17, 1835; proved Nov. 30, 1835. Daughters, Catharine Streeper and Phebe

---

[1]County Clerk's records.
[2]Records of First Presbyterian Church, Bridgeton.
[3]New Jersey Marriage Licenses.

Paul. Grandchildren, Clarence son of Catharine Streeper, and Sarah and Almarine children of Phebe Paul.

Seth, Hopewell, will Mar. 18, 1789; proved Nov. 19, 1782. Wife, Eleanor. Children, Seth, John, David, Elizabeth Hall and Eleanor Falkner. Grandchildren, Thomas and Enoch, sons of Seth; and Ira, Hannah and Mary Brooks.

Susan R. Downe, will not dated; proved Oct. 24, 1854. No relationship shown.

Thomas, Hopewell, Dec. 6, 1825; proved Sept. 30, 1829. Wife, Abigail. Children, Sheppard, Henry W., Sarah Husted, Elizabeth, Rachel, Hannah and Mary.

Daniel Husted m. Sarah Brooks, Mar. 30, 1825.[1]

William D. F., Bridgeton, will Oct. 2, 1841; proved Nov. 7, 1841. Father, Jonathan Brooks.

Zebulon, Cohansey, will Mar. 7, 1744/5; proved Feb. 3, 1748. Wife Esther. Children, John, Zebulon, Joseph and Mary.

BROWN

Ann, Stow Creek, will Nov. 10, 1831; proved Dec. 10, 1831. Children, Daniel D., Richard S., Elizabeth and Sarah.

John, Hopewell, will May 19, 1749; proved June 29, 1749. Wife, Deborah. Children, Isaac and Anna.

Mary, Hopewell, will Feb. 9, 1811; proved Jan. 6, 1812. Children, Auley, Harriet and William.

Patrick, Millville, will Oct. 27, 1824; proved July 5, 1826. Brother, John Brown.

Phebe, Stow Creek, will May 8, 1856; proved July 29, 1858. Children, Charles (dec'd), Hannah Wood and Phebe Hood. Grandchildren, Emma, Caroline, Amanda and Marcella, daughters of son Charles.

Daniel Elmer Hood m. Phebe Ewing Brown, Mar. 11, 1829.[2]

---

[1] County Clerk's records.
[4] Greenwich Presbyterian Church records.

Thomas, Hopewell, will May 20, 1760; proved Feb. 25 1761. Wife, Bathniphleath. Children, Mary, John, David, Phebe, Elizabeth, Mabell, Daniel and Thomas.

Thomas Brown m. Bathniphleath Ogden (widow), Apr. 17, 1760.

BROWNING

Jacob, Maurice River, will Oct. 12, 1794; proved Nov. 5, 1794. Wife, Margaret. Children, George, William, Mary, Rebecca, Catharine, and an expected child.

BRUFF

John, Hopewell, will Sept. 14, 1840; proved Feb. 18, 1846. Grandchildren, Jacob Johnson and Sarah Chase.

BUCK

Ephraim, Fairfield, will May 11, 1777; proved June 11, 1777. Wife, Abigail. Children, Jeremiah, Reuben, Joseph, Ephraim, Ruth and Judith.

Ephraim Buck m. Abigail Ogden, Sept. 27, 1769.[1]

John, Fairfield, will Apr. 14, 1782; proved Mar. 3, 1783. Wife, Susannah. Sons, Daton, Ephraim. Wife's daughter, Hannah Lummis.

Joseph, Millville, will Mar. 23, 1802; proved May 24, 1803. Wife, Ruth. Children, John, Ephraim, Jane and Hannah.

Joseph Buck m. Ruth Daton, Mar. 15, 1779.[1]

Sarah, Bridgeton; will Apr. 5, 1847; proved Oct. 14, 1848. Children, Robert, Francis, Jeremiah, and Sarah H.

Violetta, Bridgeton, will Mar. 29, 1837; proved July 9, 1838. Uncle, Jeremiah Buck (dec'd). Cousin, Sarah H., daughter of Jeremiah Buck.

William, Bridgeton, will Dec. 24, 1821; proved Jan. 4, 1822 Mother, Sarah Buck. Brothers and sisters, Robert, Francis Sarah H., and Jeremiah H.

---

[1]New Jersey Marriage Licenses.

BURCH

Thomas, Fairfield, will July 25, 1812; proved Aug. 1, 1812. Wife, Phebe. Children, Matthias, James, Aretas, Susannah Clark, Hannah, Ruth, Phebe and Keziah. Son-in-law Charles Clark.

BURGIN

Elizabeth, Hopewell, will Sept. 3, 1807; proved Feb. 17, 1812. Children, George, Hannah Miller, Rueben and Enoch. Grandchildren, John and George H. Burgin; John, son of Seeley Fithian; Betsey, Sally and Ruth, daughters of Reuben Burgin. Cousins, Sally Rose and Peggy Dunn.

Stephen Miller m. Hannah Burgin, May 8, 1787.[1]

Enoch, Bridgeton, will Sept. 2, 1815; proved Sept. 18, 1815. Wife, Mary. Children, David R. and Elizabeth A.

George, will Mar. 3, 1813; proved Aug. 11, 1813. Sister, Hannah Miller. Brothers, Reuben and Enoch Burgin. Nephews and neices, John, George H., Elizabeth, Sarah and Ruth, children of Reuben Burgin.

John, Hopewell, Oct. 18, 1793; proved Nov. 19, 1793. Wife, mentioned but not by name. Children, Reuben, John, Hannah Miller, Ruth Fithian, Mary, George and Enoch.

BURROUGHS

Eliza C., Millville, will Sept. 19, 1858; proved Oct. 16, 1858. Daughters, Cordelia and Charlotte. Sister, Catharine Stanly.

BURT

Jasper, Fairfield, will May 5, 1813; proved June 4, 1813. Wife, Anne. Children, Jasper, William D., Lodemy, Smith, John and Ralph.

Daniel, Fairfield, will June 8, 1841; proved Mar. 20, 1844. Children, Daniel, and Abigail Harris.

David Harris m. Abigail Burt, Apr. 6, 1825.[2]

Greenwich Presbyterian Church records.
County Clerk's records.

John, will Mar. 25, 1795; proved Mar. 31, 1801. Children, Richard, Noah, Daniel, John, Jasper, and Sarah Rulong.

John Rulon m. Sarah Burt, Dec. 10, 1782.[1]

Joseph, Cedarville, will May 17, 1831; proved July 16, 1831. Wife, half-brothers and sisters mentioned, but not by name. Sister, Charlotte Russel.

BUSBY

Isaac, Maurice River, will Apr. 2, 1803; proved June 8, 1803. Wife, Sarah. Children, Joseph, Prudence Murphy, Mary Prickett, Martha and Rachel.

BUTCHER

James, Stoe Creek, will Feb. 9, 1754; proved May 10, 1754. Wife, Mary. Daughter, Hannah. Cousin, Thomas, son of Richard Butcher. Uncle, Richard Butcher. Brother Thomas Platts.

Job, Stow Creek, will Mar. 20, 1793; proved Nov. 27, 1794. Wife, Virgin. Son, Cyrus.

Richard, Stow Creek, will Jan. 11, 1790; proved Sept. 11, 1790. Son, Job. Grandchildren, Rebecca Jeffreys, Elizabeth Ware, Jonathan, Thomas, Aaron and James Butcher.

BUTLER

John, will Aug. 26, 1770; proved Mar. 23, 1771. Wife, Elizabeth. Children, Richard, Amos, Lydia, Elizabeth, Hannah and Tabitha. Mother-in-law, Priscilla Butler.

John, Sr., Greenwich, will Mar. 5, 1769; proved Mar. 24, 1769. Wife, Priscilla. Son, John. Grandchildren, Amos and John, sons of son John; Lydia, Mary and Rachel Butler.

BUZBY

Daniel, Downe, will Sept. 19, 1816; proved Sept. 19, 1821. Wife, Ann. Children, Daniel, Joseph, Beulah Compton, Mary Compton, Meribe Hews and Hannah Compton. Granddaughters, Elizabeth

---

[1] New Jersey Marriage Licenses.

and Hannah, daughters of Hannah Compton. Brother, Joseph Buzby. Former wife's son, Jehu Buzby.

Aaron Hughes m. Maribi Buzby, Apr. 26, 1815.[1]

Nathaniel, Maurice River, will Sept. 13, 1823; proved Nov. 9, 1824. Wife, Millicent. Children, Martha, Millicent, Rebecca, Sarah, Nathaniel, William and Isaac.

CAKE

Sarah, Deerfield, will June 5, 1827; proved June 9, 1828. Son, David Royal, Daughter-in-law Rachel Royal, who has a daughter Hannah Johnson. Grandsons, David and Joel Royal.

CAMBERN

John, Millville, will Feb. 18, 1842; proved Mar. 17, 1842. Wife's daughter, Mary Ann. First wife's children, Ann, Nathan, Sarah and Robert.

CAMPBELL

John, Downe, will Apr. 8, 1832; proved Apr. 25, 1832. Wife, Sophia. Children, Archibald, Elizabeth Robbins, William and John.

David Robbins m. Elizabeth Campbell, Jan. 2, 1814.[1]

Robert, will Nov. 11, 1748; proved Feb. 23, 1748/9. Wife, Mary. Sons, Robert and William.

Thomas, will May 19, 1795; proved June 8, 1795. Wife, Mary Children mentioned, but not by name.

CARLL

Esther P., Bridgeton, will March 28, 1860; proved Dec. 22, 1860. Husband, Ephraim Carll (dec'd). Children, Robert B., Richard D. and Hiram D. Carll. Daughter-in-law, Emily, wife of son Richard.

Mary Ann. Bridgeton, Feb. 10, 1859; proved Feb. 23, 1859. Sons, Francis and Eli.

---

[1] County Clerk's records.

Phineas, Greenwich, will Jan. 18, 1806; proved Mar. 16, 1806. Wife, Hannah. Children, Betsy, Maskell, George and Thomas.

William, Greenwich, will Sept. 20, 1773; proved Oct. 11, 1773. Daughter, Rebekah. (Borton and Buckley Carll and Sarah Ewing mentioned, but relationship not given.)

CASPER

Luarence, Hopewell, Oct. 18, 1809; proved Mar. 3, 1810. Children, Adam, Philip, Mary, Catherine wife of Jacob Hoover, and Laurence. Grandchildren, Peter and Samuel. sons of Jacob Hoover; and Laurence Shriner and Sarah Casper.

Philip, Hopewell, will July 26, 1834; proved Sept. 5, 1834. Wife, Susanna. Sons, Asa and Philip.

CASTO

William, Deerfield, will July 22, 1777; proved Aug. 26, 1778. Wife, Sarah. Children, Abel, Azariah, Elizabeth Kille, John, Andrew, David, Jonathan, Jeremiah, William, Jacob, Thomas and Abijah.

CHAMBERS

John, Maurice River, Apr. 18. 1836; proved June 30, 1836. Wife, Abigail. Children, Jeremiah, Robert, and Sarah Peterson.

William, will Dec. 24, 1804; proved Feb. 25, 1805. Wife, Elizabeth. Sons, Daniel, Jeremiah, John and Robert.

CHANCE

John, Maurice River, will June 28, 1828; proved June 8, 1829. Wife, Sarah. Children, Mary Chambers, Walton, Elizabeth Hoffman, Sarah Robinson. Grandchildren, John and Asa Chance, Unice Hunter, Elizabeth and Hannah Chambers, Jeremia son of Walton Chance, Jonathan and Elizabeth Hoffman, and John and Steelman Robinson.

Elkanah Robinson m. Sarah Chance, Aug. 8, 1821.[1]

---

[1]County Clerk's records.

CHARD

Benjamin, Downe, will Mar. 9, 1793; proved July 4, 1793. Children, Sarah Harmer, and William.

Hugh, will Oct. 12, 1794; proved Nov. 8, 1794. Children, Joel, Hannah Claypoole, Mary, and Elizabeth Tumbleson.

Theodocia, Fairfield, will Jan. 4, 1834; proved Mar. 28, 1837. Children, William Preston, Violetta, Abigail and Theodosia.

William, Downe, will Mar. 1, 1817; proved Apr. 17, 1817. Daughter, Elizabeth Taylor. Grandchildren, Charlotte and Betsey Kimsey, William J., Mary and Ann Chard. Daughter-in-law, Rececca Kimsey.

Jonathan Taylor m. Elizabeth Chard, Dec. 25, 1800.[1]

CHARLESWORTH

William, Millville, will Mar. 26, 1849; proved Apr. 19, 1849. Children Mary, Garrison, James and John. Grandchildren, Elizabeth, Ruth, Ellen and John, children of son John.

CHURCH

Silas, Fairfield, Apr. 7, 1761; proved Apr. 22, 1761. Wife, Martha. Children, Joseph, Christopher. Deborah and Alice. Father, John Page. Brother-in-law, Benjamin Stites.

CLARK

Arthur, Hopewell, Apr. 23, 1817; proved July 8, 1817. Wife, Mary. Children, James, John, Elizabeth, Sarah, Thomas D., Arthur, Uriah and Nicholas.

Daniel, Hopewell, will Dec. 12, 1774; proved Jan. 11, 1775. Wife, Rachel. Children, Daniel, Charles, Mary, Anne and Phebe. Brother-in-law, Abijah Holmes.

Elizabeth, Greenwich, will Oct. 8, 1760; proved Dec. 2, 1760. Children, Susanna Stathem and Elizabeth Penton. Nephew, John Reves.

---

[1]County Clerk's records.

James, Fairfield, will Apr. 27, 1784; proved Sept. 25, 1789. Wife, Sarah. Children, James, David, Rhoda, Mary, Ruth and Bathsheba.

James, Fairfield, will Aug. 25, 1829; proved Nov. 14, 1832. Wife, Sarah.

Joel, will Mar. 27, 1801; proved Apr. 15, 1801. Wife, Ann. Sisters, Elizabeth Dollas and Mary Busby.

John, Cohansie, will Feb. 7, 1786; proved Feb. 20, 1786. Brother, Alexander Clark. Sister, Isabella Clark. Sister-in-law, Elizabeth Smith.

Sarah, Fairfield, will May 5, 1849; proved May 19, 1851. Grandchildren, Ellen L. Seward, Elvira J., Mary D. and W. Lewis Githens.

Stephen, Downe, will Apr. 10, 1778; proved May, 1781. Wife' Deborah. Children, James, Stephen and Nathan. Grandchildren, Charles and John, sons of Stephen.

COBB

Erick, will Feb. 11, 1781; proved Mar. 3, 1781. Wife, Rodah. Children, Samuel, Joshua, Judah; Tabitha and Anne.

John, will Mar. 25, 1783; proved July 14, 1784. Wife, Sarah. Children, John, Aamos, Jonathan, and Sarah Wickward. Cozen, Georg Armstrong.

John, Downe, will June 5, 1837; proved July 12, 1858. Wife, Esther. Sister, Jennie Cobb. Nephew, Charles, son of Jennie Cobb.

Paul, will Feb. 15, 1767; proved July 16, 1767. Wife mentioned, but not by name. Children, Joshua, William, Calop, Paul and Theodors.

Sarah (widow of John), Downe, will Apr. 7, 1799; proved June 15, 1799. Children, John, and Sarah Wickward. Grandson Thomas Cobb.

CODDINGTON

Benjamin, Greenwich, will Jan. 5, 1792; proved Apr. 3, 1793. Wife, Phebe. Children, John, Moses, William, Phebe and Rhoda.

CODE

John, Bridgeton, will Sept. 27, 1833; proved Sept. 26, 1835. Wife, Rebecca. Children, Mary Pew, Eleanor Bowen, John and Westley.

COLLINGS

William, Greenwich, will Jan. 14, 1761; proved Nov. 5, 1762. Wife, Elizabeth. Brother, Richard Collins. Wife's uncle and aunt, Humphry and Phebe Fithian.

COMPTON

Gilbert, Downe, will Dec. 30, 1841; proved Feb. 13, 1843. Children, Abigail wife of Allen Shinn, Elizabeth, Sarah, Joseph, Gilbert, Samuel, James, David, Mary Sharp (dec'd) and Nancy Lore (dec'd).

Ichabod, Down, will Jan. 5, 1833; proved Feb. 11, 1833. Children, Charles, Daniel B., George E. and Joseph.

CONEY

Jonathan, Millville, will 1828; proved Apr. 30, 1830. Wife, Esther. Children, Martha A., Jane S., David S., Sarah Edwards, and Jonathan.

CONNER

Henry W., Cedarville, will not dated; proved July 5, 1860. Wife, Rebecca. Children and grandchildren mentioned, but not by name.

Mary, Fairfield, will Aug. 6, 1842; proved Feb. 15, 1849. Children, Darcus, Thomas, Judah Morrison, Ann Jackson and Caroline Stratton.

Jethro Jackson m. Ann Conner, Apr. 8, 1830.[1]

William Morrison m. Judith Conner, June 29, 1829.[1]

---

[1] County Clerk's records.

COOK

Eldad, will Oct. 25, 1782; proved May 25, 1786. Wife, Deborah. Children, Abel, Eldad, David, John, Rachel, Phebe, Martha and Mary.

Eldad, Stow Creek, will Apr. 8, 1809; proved May 27, 1809. Wife, Rachel. Children, Elizabeth, Hannah, Rachel, Zacheus, Eldad and William.

Jonathan, Stow Creek, will May 25, 1830; proved Feb. 2, 1831. Wife, Abigail. Brother, David Cook. Nephew, David Cook, Jr.

Rachel (widow), Stow Creek, will Feb. 10, 1817; proved Jan. 16, 1822. Children, Elizabeth, Hannah, Eldad, William, Rachel and Zacheus.

COOMBS

Jesse, Millville, will Oct. 12, 1846; proved Nov. 5, 1846. Wife, Mary. Children, Jacob, Joshua, Jesse, David, Samuel, John, Ruth wife of James M. Riley, Elizabeth wife of Stephen Garrison, Mary wife of Theodore B. Higby, Jane Ann and Christiana.

Stephen Garrison m. Elizabeth Coombs, Mar. 31, 1830.[1]

Theodore Higbee m. Mary Coombs, Apr. 21, 1835.[1]

CORNWELL

John, Deerfield, will June 9, 1785; proved June 13, 1795. Children, Jonathan, Hannah Garrison, David, Sarah Sheets, Phebe Joslin, Mary Bigs, William and Abigail.

Jonathan, Deerfield, will May 4, 1822; proved Mar. 24, 1827. Wife, Dorcas. Children, Philip, Lot, Jonathan, Hannah Garrison, Dorcas, and Kittary Sayre. Son-in-law, Arthur Garrison.

William Sayre m. Kitheriah Cornwell, Aug. 5, 1809.[1]

CORSON

Andrew, Maurice River, will Sept. 12, 1791; proved Nov. 26, 1792. Son, Andrew. Grandchildren, Silvia Drummond, Isaac Corson, Abel and Hannah Steelman.

---

[1] County Clerk's records.

COTTING

Elias, Hopewell, will Nov. 23, 1757; proved Jan. 7, 1758. Wife, Elizabeth. Children, Elizabeth James and Mary Bower(or Bowen)¡

COX

Samuel, Maurice River, will Mar. 8, 1855; proved Apr. 22, 1856 Children, Sarah Clark, Mary Trout, Samuel, Rachel Errickson, Phebe Shropshire, Jonathan, Elias, Andrew, and Rebecca D. Weldon.
Jeremiah Clark m. Sarah Cox, Dec. 28, 1822.[1]
Silsby Errickson m. Rachel Cox, Feb. 1, 1834.[1]
Bennett Shropshire m. Phebe Cox, Mar. 2, 1833.[1]

COZIER

Benjamin, Downe, Dec. 20, 1838; proved Oct. 23, 1850. Children, Jonathan, Dolly Hanna, Elizabeth Shaw and Naomi Bowen.

CRAVEN

Nehemiah, will Apr. 22, 1749; proved May 10, 1749. Children, Thomas and Mary.

CRESE

Aaron, will May 13, 1802; proved Oct. 8, 1802. Children, Josiah, and Elizabeth Bowen. Grandchildren, Deborah and Sarah Bowen.

CROKER

Daniel, Greenwich, Apr. 1, 1853; proved July 25, 1854. Wife, Henrietta. Son, Harrison. Granddaughter, Henrietta Smith.

CROSLEY

Moses, Fairfield, will Apr. 30, 1759; proved May 21, 1759. Wife, Sarah. Children, Bethnia wife of Jacob Golder, Hannah, Rachel Harris and Abraham. Grandsons, Moses, Aaron and George Crosley. Son-in-law, Jacob Harris.

---

[1]County Clerk's records.

DANZENBAKER

George, Hopewell, will June 15, 1832; proved Sept. 4, 1832. Wife, Elizabeth. Children, Mary (daughter by last wife); others mentioned, but not by name.

Jacob, Fairfield, will May 5, 1858; proved Aug. 9, 1858. Wife, Sarah.

DANZENBECHER

Lewis, will Feb. 15, 1806; proved July 17, 1809. Children, Elizabeth, Lewis, Jacob and George.

DARE

Abiel, will June 26, 1775; proved June 12, 1777. Wife and daughters mentioned, but not by name. Sons, Joseph and Reuben.

Benjamin, Hopewell, will Mar. 20, 1837; proved Aug. 7, 1837. Wife, Mary. Sons, Samuel and Lewis. Grandchildren, Mulford and George, sons of Samuel; Benjamin and James, sons of Lewis; Rebecca, wife of Archibald Woodruff; and Mary, wife of Alpheus Brooks. Neice Harriet, wife of James Sheppard.

Benoni, Greenwich, will Dec. 16, 1768; proved Aug. 14 1770. Wife, Clemens. Children, Elkanah, William, Abel, Reuben, James, Elanor, Elizabeth and Rachel. Grandchildren, Benoni, Elkanah, Annes, John, Benjamin, Prudence Hall and David Long.
Benoni Dare m. Clemens Waithman, May 9, 1760.[1]

Daniel, Deerfield, will Aug. 7, 1781; proved Dec. 13, 1782. Wife mentioned, but not by name. Children, Daniel, Benjamin, Ludlam, Ruth, Mara, Phebe, Sarah, Amy, Abigail and Lydia.

Edmund, Stoe Creek, will June 29, 1849; proved Feb. 16, 1849. Children, William, Charles, James, Edmund, and Sarah wife of David Minch (formerly wife of Jonathan S. Ayars).
Jonathan Ayres m. Sarah Dare, May 23, 1838.[2]
David Minch m Mrs. Sarah Ayars, Jan. 28, 1843.[2]

---

[1]New Jersey Marriage Licenses.
[2]County Clerk's records.

Eli, Deerfield, will June 16, 1809; proved July 24, 1809. Wife, Laticia. Son, James Smith. Brother, John Dare.

Elizabeth, Fairfield, will July 25, 1755; proved Jan. 30, 1756. Children, Jonathan and Nathan Lorance, Violotta Harris, Abigail Elmer, Elizabeth Shepherd and Rhoda Johnson.

Elkanah, Cohansey, will Mar. 17, 1752; proved Apr. 28, 1759, Elizabeth. Children, Benoni, Elkana, and six daughters mentioned but not by name.

Hannah, Deerfield, will Apr. 27, 1795; proved Nov. 4, 1795. Children, Mary, Hannah, Susannah and Sarah.

John, Deerfield, will Sept. 18, 1785; proved Nov. 25, 1785. Wife, Christian. Children, John, Philip, Seeley, William, Hannah, Elizabeth and Sarah.

Jonathan, Deerfield, will Oct. 4, 1838; proved Oct. 25, 1838. Children, Lydia Ann, Jonathan, Dayton, Emeline, Eliza, Frances Mulford, Mary Elizabeth, Ephraim H. and Mary Jane.

Jonathan, Bridgeton, July 14, 1848; proved Nov. 17, 1849. Brother, Ephraim H. Dare. Sisters, Sarah Jane and Mary Elizabeth Dare.

Ludlam, Deerfield, will Nov. 29, 1827; proved Aug. 11, 1830. Children, Ludlam, Rhoda, Daniel, Azuba Parvin and Ruth D. Shull. Grandson, George Caruthers.

Rachel, Deerfield, will Jan. 1, 1821; proved May 10, 1821. Grandchildren, Mary, Nancy, Julian and James Cake; Rachel, daughter of John Dare and granddaughter of Philip Dare.

Rebecca, Bridgeton, will July 11, 1840; proved Aug. 19, 1842. Children, John Dare, Elizabeth Woodruff, Leonard Dare and Rebecca Garrison.

Reuben, Greenwich, will Aug. 31, 1776; proved Sept. 25, 1777. Wife, Rebecca. Children mentioned, but not by name.

Robert, Deerfield, will May 24, 1789; proved Sept. 23, 1789. Wife, Mary. Sons Robert, Jeremiah, John and Gamaliel. Daughters mentioned, but not by name.

Seeley, Deerfield, Sept. 14, 1811; proved Sept. 21, 1811. Wife Hannah. Son-in-law, Martin Synnott.

William, Cohansey, will Feb. 1, 1747/8; proved Dec. 6, 1749. Wife, Elizabeth. Children, William, John, Mary Jessop, Hannah Ogden, Elizabeth Preston, Rachel Westcott and Sarah Westcott.

William, Deerfield, will Dec. 12, 1759; proved Mar. 7, 1760. Wife, Hannah. Children, William, Levi, Jonathan, Mary Bowen, Abigail, Freelove, Rachel and Amey.

DATEN

Eli, Fairfield, will Apr. 4, 1775; proved May 17, 1775. Wife, Abigail. Daughter, Ann. Father, Joseph Daten. Brothers, Leonard and Henry Daten.

Freelove (widow of Joseph), Fairfield, will Aug. 11, 1789; proved Nov. 6, 1789. Children, Ephraim, Mary, Sarah, Freelove and Joseph. Grandson, Joseph Daten.

DATON

Joseph, Fairfield, will Sept. 2, 1770; proved Dec. 14, 1770. Wife, Prudence. Children, Leonard, Joseph, Eli, Henry, Mary and Anne.

Sarah, Bridgeton, will Jan. 22, 1777; proved June 16, 1777. Grandchildren, Patience Terry, and Ephraim Terry who has sons Andrew and Josiah.

DATTEN

David, Fairfield, will Feb. 6, 1770; proved Feb. 28, 1770. Wife, Ann. Children, David, Hannah and Ruth.

DAVIS

Arthur, Deerfield, will Nov. 5, 1788; proved Dec. 11, 1789. Wife, Esther. Children, Elijah, Daniel, Arthur, Martha Ogden, Ruth Garrison, Naomy Shull, Benjamin and Abijah. Grandson, Arthur, son of Arthur Davis.

Barzilla, Stoe Creek, will Aug. 20, 1837; proved Sept. 4, 1837. Children mentioned, but not by name. Brother, Reuben Davis.

Benjamin, Deerfield, will Feb. 16, 1836; proved Mar. 13, 1837. Wife, Deborah. Children, Benjamin, Esther P. Carll, Jane Bush and Alfred.

Broadway, Deerfield, will Sept. 9, 1845; proved Aug. 4, 1846. Children, Lewis, Reuben, Ruth Moore, Lydia Harris and Rebecca Paulin.
Enos Harris m. Lydia Davis, Jan. 18, 1816.[1]

Daniel, Deerfield, will Jan. 3, 1758; proved Feb. 14, 1763. Wife, Deborah. Children, Bradway, Uriah, Mary Brooks, Patience Miller, Amon, Hannah, Joseph and Arthur.

Daniel, Deerfield, will not dated; proved Dec. 11, 1805. Children, Elijah, Daniel, Rheuma and Jemima. Grandchildren, Aaron and Hannah Davis, and Rebecca and Hannah Stratton.

David, Hopewell, will Sept. 16, 1842; proved July 15, 1844. Wife, Naomi. Children, Edith Sheppard, Hannah Davis, Annie Sheppard, Anna Davis, Naomi Wood, and Margaret F. Randolph. Granddaughter, Rebecca Frazure (nee White.)
Caleb Sheppard m. Edith Davis, June 20. 1816.[2]
Lewis Wood m. Naomi Davis, Oct. 30, 1821.[2]
Charles F. Randolph m. Margaret Davis, Oct. 30, 1821.[2]
John Frazier m. Rebecca White, Mar. 3, 1834.[2]

Ebenezer, Hopewell, Apr. 24, 1825; proved Mar. 3, 1827, Wife Margaret. Children, Jane, John T., James and Ebenezer.

Elijah, will Aug. 20, 1810; proved Aug. 30, 1810. Wife, Patience.

Elizabeth, Stow Creek, ¦Aug. 13, 1830; proved Feb. 18, 1831. Children, Abigail Sheppard, Dickason, Isaac and Beulah.
William T. Sheppard m. Abigail A. Davis, Dec. 12, 1828.[2]

Elnathan, Hopewell, Aug. 25, 1771; proved July 30, 1773. Children, Elnathan, Job, Ruth, Phebe, Mary, Jemima and Nathan.

Elnathan will Dec. 8, 1802; proved Dec. 31, 1802. Wife, Susannah. Children, Susannah, Margaret Sheppard, Jonathan, Jacob, Ebenezer, Jedidiah, Samuel B. and Elnathan. Grandchildren, Ruth, daughter of Richard Davis, and Jeremiah and Ruth, children

---
[1]Records of First Presbyterian Church, Bridgeton.
[2]County Clerk's records.

of Jeremiah Davis.   Daughter-in-law, Martha, widow of son Jeremiah.

Gabriel, Greenwich, will Jan. 25, 1797; proved Oct. 2, 1798. Wife, Sarah. Relations, Bathsheba, wife of Daniel Smith; Susannah, wife of Daniel Murphey; Charles, son of Charles Bacon; David R. Morrow; Sarah, wife of Mark Hall, and Hannah, wife of Benjamin Acton. Nephews or cousins, Ebenezer and Abel Hall.

Hannah, Hopewell, will May 10, 1841; proved Mar. 28, 1842. Daughter, Mary, wife of Lewis Davis. Grandchildren, James, Sheppard and Thomas.

James, Deerfield, will Sept. 11, 1777; proved Dec. 18, 1780. Wife, Mary. Children, Jonathan, Abishua, Othniel, James, David, Sarah, Rachel, Johannah, Elizabeth and Esther. Brother, Arthur Davis. Granddaughter, Mary, daughter of Jonathan.

James, Bridgeton, will Dec. 1, 1847; proved Jan. 11, 1855. Wife, Rebecca. Children, Isaac C., Arthur, James J., Rebecca, wife of James Nichols, and Nicholas. Adopted daughter, Harriet, wife of Samuel Benson.

Jedidiah, Hopewell, will Jan. 14, 1829; proved Mar. 18, 1829. Wife, Ammorilla. Children, Rebecca Harris, Matilda A. Shull and Rachel B. Brooks. Son-in-law, William Shull.

John, Deerfield, will Apr. 11, 1838; proved May 24, 1838. Wife, Sarah. Children, Ephraim B., Elizabeth E., Anna L., Rebecca, Phebe, John L., Joseph L. and Susan.

John, Hopewell, will July 11, 1851; proved Aug. 18, 1854. Wife, Jane. Children, David, Amos S., Enoch James, Edward, James M., Lewis, John B., Phebe Bidwell, and Susan Jane Bowen. Grandchildren, Henry Clay and Mary Eliza, children of son David.

George Bidwell m. Phebe Davis, Dec. 1, 1836.[1]

Thomas Bowen m. Susan Jane Davis, Sept. 9, 1841.[1]

Jonathan, Cohansey, will Aug. 15, 1764; proved Feb. 21 1769. Wife, Esther. Children, Jarman, Elnathan, Naomi and Edith, wife of Benjamin Dunn.

---

[1] County Clerk's records.

Jonathan, will May 26, 1784; proved Aug. 19, 1785. Wife, Margaret. Children, Samuel, David. Richard, John, Ammi, Sarah Thomas and Anna.

Jonathan, Stow Creek, will Feb. 1, 1817; proved Sept. 20, 1819. Children, Lewis, George, Jonathan, Ephraim, Reese, Beulah, Sarah Ayars, Susanna and Elkanah.

Amasa Ayars m. Sarah Davis, Nov. 22, 1814.[1]

Levi, Fairfield, will Nov. 7, 1799; proved Apr. 6, 1802. Nephews, Levi Dare, Ephraim, son of sister Freelove Daton, and Joseph, son of Ephraim Daton.

Lewis, Hopewell, will Oct. 5, 1846; proved Apr. 12, 1852. Wife, Mary H. Children, Melisa, wife of Dickason Sheppard, and Hannah L.

Dicason Sheppard m. Malissa B. Davis, Feb. 8, 1834.[2]

Mary H., Hopewell, will Apr. 23, 1852; proved Aug. 25, 1854. Son-in-law, Dickenson Sheppard.

Othniel, will Sept. 14, 1799; proved Feb. 17, 1808. Nephews, Charles and Jeremiah, sons of Abishai Davis; Edmund and David, sons of David Davis. Neices, Sarah, Hannah and Ruth, daughters of brother James and Ruth Davis; and Mary, daughter of sister Esther Ireland.

Patience, will not dated; proved Oct. 27, 1813. Nephew and neices, Samuel Thompson, Hester Burch, Elizabeth Reeve and Abigail Cake.

Samuel, Stow Creek, will Aug. 30, 1785; proved Oct. 31, 1785. Children Samuel, Isaac, Elijah, Evan and Reuben.

Samuel, Hopewell, will June 3, 1833; proved Mar. 10, 1834. Wife, Hannah (late Hannah Sheppard). Children, Abel, Howell, Anne Ayres, Eliza, Sarah Perry (late Frazeur), dec'd, and Mary High. Grandson, Samuel D., son of Mary High.

Enoch Ayars m. Anna Davis, July 17, 1797.[2]
David Frazer m. Sarah Davis, Dec. 25, 1805.[2]
Jeremiah Perry m. Sarah Frazier, Aug. 8, 1822.[2]

---

[1]Salem County Clerk's records.
[2]County Clerk's records.

Samuel, Stoe Creek, will Apr. 25, 1846; proved May 19, 1846. Wife, Abigail. Children, Dorris A., Isaac, John W., Azel, Lucy West, George B. and Henry W.

Richard West m. Lucy Davis, Oct. 18, 1832.[1]

Sarah (widow of Gabriel), will not dated; proved May 4, 1805. Cousins, Joseph Harmer, Ebenezer M., son of Moses Hall, and Thomas and Charles Bacon.

Susannah, will May 14, 1805; proved Apr. 30, 1810. Children, Susannah, Margaret Sheppard, Jedediah, Jacob, Jonathan, Ebenezer, Samuel B. and Elnathan. Grandchildren, Jeremiah and Ruth, children of Jeremiah Davis; Levi and Elizabeth Davis.

Dickeson Sheppard m. Margaret Davis, Jan. 8, 1800.[1]

Susannah, Stoe Creek, will July 14, 1833; proved Sept. 11, 1837. Children, Reuben, Jr., Jane Peck, Margaret, Hannah, Maria, Susanna Bond and Anna Sheppard.

Thomas Peck m. Jane Davis, Jan. 16, 1823.[1]

Uriah, Deerfield, will Oct. 10, 1799; proved Aug. 3, 1805. Wife, Sarah. Children, Enos, Uriah, Damaris, Sarah and Esther. Son-in-law, James Westcott. Granddaughter, Rachel Miller.

James Westcott m. Damaris Davis, Mar. 20, 1792.[2]

Uriah, Deerfield, will Apr. 3, 1819; proved Feb. 18, 1820. Wife, Elizabeth. Children, Aaron, Hannah Harris, Susanna, Patience T. and Phebe G. Granddaughters, Cynthia and Rachel Reeves.

Ephraim Harris m. Hannah Davis, Nov. 30, 1816.[1]

DAYTON

Ephraim, Fairfield, will Jan. 16, 1810; proved Feb. 20, 1810. Wife, Margarette. Children, Joseph, Ephraim and Rachel.

Joseph, Fairfield, will Dec. 19, 1777; proved Jan. 13, 1779. Wife, Freelove. Children, Mary, Sarah and Freelove.

---

[1]County Clerk's records.
[2]Fairfield Presbyterian Church records.

DENN

Joseph, Stoe Creek, will Oct. 16, 1752; proved Dec. 4, 1752. Wife, Rebeckah. Expected child. Cousins, Amos and Joseph, sons of Daniel and Mary Bacon.

DENNEY

Esther, Greenwich, will Apr. 10, 1812; proved Apr. 15, 1812. Children, John Richerson, Richard Richerson, Joseph Denney, William Richerson, Robert Richerson, and Priscilla.

DENNIS

Elizabeth, will Apr. 18, 1782; proved Mar. 13, 1788. Brother William Miller. Aunt, Lucy Dennis. Cousins, Hannah, Philip and Jonathan Dennis, and David Denn.

Hannah, Greenwich, will Feb. 25, 1799; proved May 8, 1805. Children, Sarah, and Deborah Newbold. Brother-in-law, Thomas Daniel. Nephew, Samuel Newbold.

Joseph, Hopewell, will, Mar. 12, 1771; proved Sept. 6, 1771. Sister, Elizabeth Dennis. Brother, Samuel Dennis.

Mary, will Jan. 27, 1797; proved Dec. 4, 1798. Daughter, Mary. Brothers, Edward and Philip Dennis. Sister, Hannah Rulon. Neice, Elizabeth, daughter of brother Edward. Brother-in-law Nathaniel Rulon.

Philip, Greenwich, will May 1, 1767; proved May 28, 1768. Wife, Lucy. Children, Philip, Jonathan, Prudence, Elizabeth, Grace Bowen and Rachel Smith.
Philip Dennis m. Luce Bacon, Oct. 28, 1723.[1]

Philip, Greenwich, will Feb. 4, 1795; proved June 18, 1796. Wife, Hannah. Children, Mary, Hannah Rulon, Rachel, Sarah, Edward, John and Philip.

DENTON

William, will Mar. 3, 1752; proved Aug. 4, 1752. Wife, Ann. Children, Elena, wife of William Tullis, and Mary.

---

[1]Salem Friends' Meeting records.

DIAMENT

Hedges, Downe, will Dec. 9. 1776. Brothers, Jonathan, Nathaniel and James. Sisters, Sarah Swing, Dorcas Peterson and Rhoda Diament.

James, Fairfield, will Mar. 1, 1776; proved Apr. 19, 1776. Children, James, Sarah wife of John Westcott, Abigail wife of Charles Howell, Nathaniel, Hannah, Mary, Ruth and Louis (Louise?)

James, Jones Island, will Jan. 9, 1841; proved Sept. 5, 1845. Wife, Bathsheba. Children, James, Nathaniel, Elmer (dec'd), Sarah Alderman, Theodosia (dec'd) wife of John Henderson, Ruth Fithian, Rosina wife of Preston Foster, Jane E. Bateman and Hannah Newcomb. Grandson, Theophilus E. Diament. Son-in-law, Isaac Newcomb.

Daniel B. Stretch m. Theodosia Diament, Mar. 12, 1812.[1]
John Henderson m. Theodosia (Diament) Stretch, June 4, 1816.[1]
Joseph Fithian m. Ruth Diament, Jan. 1. 1812.[1]
Isaac P. Foster m. Rosina Diament, Nov. 22, 1816.[1]
Harvey Bateman m. Jane Diament, June 4, 1826.[1]
Isaac Newcomb m. Hannah Diament, Nov. 22, 1816.[1]

Jonathan, Jones Island, will Mar. 6, 1798; proved Dec. 10, 1805. Wife, Sarah. First wife's son, David Harris.

Lois, Fairfield, will Nov. 7, 1769; proved Dec. 31, 1770. Children, Hedges, Jonathan, James, Nathaniel, Lois Bennit, Sarah Swing, Dorcas, Elizabeth and Rhoda.

Nathaniel, will Apr. 23, 1766; proved May 14, 1767. Wife, Lowis. Children Jonathan, James, Nathaniel, Hedges, Lowis Bennit, Sarah Swing, Dorcas, Elizabeth, Ruth Powell and Roda.

Nathaniel, Fairfield, will Jan. 25, 1820; proved Nov. 27, 1821. Grandchildren, Benjamin J. Diament and Elizabeth Smith.

DIXON

Daniel, Fairfield, will Aug. 13, 1787; proved Mar. 10, 1789. Wife, Hannah. Children, Urban, Mary, Elizabeth and Tamson. Grandchildren, Daniel and Mary Dixon.

---

[1]County Clerk's records.

FROM CUMBERLAND COUNTY WILLS

Daniel, Fairfield, will Dec. 5, 1842; proved Dec. 31, 1842. Children, Daniel, Hannah H. Jarl, Mary Jane, Sarah Ann and Harriet. Bower Jerrel m. Hannah H. Dixon, May 1, 1841.[1]

DOLLES

William, Downe, will Jan. 12, 1784; proved Apr. 27, 1784. Children, William, Samuel, Elizabeth Bright and Reuben. Grandchildren, Mary Dollas, Dollas Lore and Hezekiah Lore. Son-in-law, William Bright.

DONNELLY

William, Maurice River, will Aug. 1, 1784; proved Sept. 23, 1784. Wife, Catharine. Children, John, George, Nancy and Lettice.

DORTON

George, Hopewell, will Feb. 18, 1835; proved Mar. 16, 1835. Brothers, Alfred, Henry and Ephraim.

DOWDNEY

John, Hopewell, will Feb. 17, 1758; proved Mar. 22, 1858. Wife, Tabitha. Children, Nicholas, Nathaniel, John, Burrows, George and Mary.

DOWNAM

William, Fairfield, will Dec. 27, 1845; proved Aug. 12, 1846. Wife, Rachel. Children, Elizabeth H., Leonard, Henry H., Martha, Ann and Rachel.

DUFFIELD

William, Fairfield, will June 27, 1843; proved May 1, 1848. Wife, Mary. Sons, William, and Nathan. Grandsons, William, Franklin and Albert, sons of William.

---

[1]County Clerk's records.

DUNDERGILL

John, Hopewell, will May 20, 1857; proved June 6, 1857. Wife, Mary.

DUNHAM

David, will Oct. 12, 1841; proved Nov. 17 1841. Wife, Rachel Children, William, Mary, Susannah, Ruth Ann, Nancy W. and David L.

DUNN

Hugh, Stow Creek, will Jan. 1, 1759; proved July 10, 1759. Wife, Amey. Children, Hugh, Amey Dunham, Samuel, Zurviah Barratt, Keziah Ayars, Mary Riel and Sarah Davis.
Joseph Ayars m. Keziah Dunn, Nov. 27, 1738.[1]

ELKINTON

Beulah, Downe, will Nov. 18, 1839; proved Feb. 19, 1845. Nephews and neices, George Elkinton; Aden, and Elizabeth Compton, children of brother David Wills; Daniel, son of Samuel Wills; Beulah, Aquilla, John and Daniel, children of brother James Wills; Daniel, son of sister Mary Buzby. Husband's brother, John Elkinton. Husband's neice, Ann Evans. David, George and Edward, sons of Ann Evans.

George, Downe, will Oct. 1, 1820; proved Nov. 6, 1820. Wife, Beulah. Wife's neices, Mary, daughter of Daniel and Mary Compton; Elizabeth Compton, daughter of James and Elizabeth Wells; Sarah Lore, daughter of John and Rhoda Elkinton, and Ann Evans, daughter of sister Hannah.

John, Port Elizabeth, will Aug. 14, 1842; proved Mar. 20, 1843. Wife mentioned but not by name. Children, Harriet Butcher (dec'd), Rhoda Taylor (dec'd), Stephen P., John A., Sarah Lore, and Ann D. C. Thompson (dec'd).

---

[1]Miscellaneous Biographies.

ELMER

Abigail (widow of Daniel), Fairfield, will Apr. 9, 1770; proved Oct. 11, 1770. Children, Abigail, widow of James Ray, Daniel, Jonathan, Timothy, Ebenezer, Deborah, wife of Lot Fithian, Victorina and Violetta.

Benjamin T., Fairfield, will Mar. 27, 1840; proved June 26, 1840. Sister, Esther Bateman. Nephews, Charles E., George and Andrew J. Elmer. Neices, Martha P. Elmer; and Martha Ann, daughter of brother Charles Elmer.

Charles Bateman m. Esther Elmer, Mar. 5, 1806.[1]

Daniel, will June 30, 1753; proved Jan. 21, 1755. Wife, Susanna. Children, Theophilus, Theodorus, Silvanus, Margaret Loomis, Samuel, Elizabeth, Rumolla and Mary. Grandchildren, Jason and Elmer Ogden, sons of daughter Mary, and Ephraim Dayton, son of daughter Ruhamaleo.

Daniel, Fairfield, will Apr. 9, 1761; proved June 26, 1761. Wife, Abigail. Children, Jonathan, Timothy, Ebenezer, Violetta, Abigail, wife of James Ray, Deborah and Victorina.

Daniel, Fairfield, will July 24, 1792; proved Nov. 15, 1792. Wife, Hester. Sons, Daniel and Charles.

Daniel, Bridgeton, will Feb. 4, 1847; proved Aug. 8, 1848. Children, Charles E. and Martha. Nephews and neices, Charles, William, Benjamin and Esther Bateman and Abigail E. B. Lawrence.

Ebenezer, Bridgeton, will June 17, 1839; proved Nov. 6, 1843. Children, Sarah, wife of Rev. Dr. William Neill, and Lucius Q. C.

Eli, Bridgeton, will Sept. 22, 1803; proved June 19, 1805. Wife, Jane. Children, Eli T.; other children mentioned, but not by name.

Horace, Cedarville, will Feb. 6, 1838; proved May 24, 1838. Wife, Phebe. Brother, John Elmer.

John, Deerfield, will Jan. 29, 1813; proved Feb. 24, 1813. Wife, Ruth. Sister Betsey.

---

[1] County Clerk's records.

John, will July 29, 1854; proved July 15, 1855. Sons, Horace and Francis.

Jonathan, Bridgeton, will Jan. 1. 1817; proved Apr. 25, 1817. Children, Elizabeth and William.

Ruth, Bridgeton, will May 1, 1821; proved Nov. 29, 1823. Sister, Mary, wife of Othnial Johnson.

Timothy, Fairfield, will Dec. 27, 1779; proved Oct. 5, 1780. Wife, Mary. Children, Timothy, Oliver and Jane. Sister, Abigail, wife of James Ray.

Timothy, Bridgeton, will Mar. 10, 1836; proved Mar. 30, 1836. Wife, Ruth. Children, George W., Jeremiah B., Timothy, Mary Jane, Joseph H. and Albert B.

William, will May 5, 1836; proved May 17, 1836. Wife, Margaret K. Children, Jonathan, William, David P., Benjamin Franklin, Mary and Nancy P.

ELWELL

David, Hopewell, will May 2, 1800; proved Sept. 24, 1800. Children, Jecamlntie Brooks, Susannah, Dolley Brooks, and David.

Jacob, Stoe Creek, will Apr. 9. 1817; proved July 8, 1817. Wife, Phebe. Children, Samuel (dec'd), David Jeremiah, William, Hannah Andrews, Rachel Ayers and Delilah Allen. Grandchildren, David, Mahlon, Jeremiah and William, sons of Samuel; Joseph, Ralph and Rebecca, children of daughter Delilah Allen. Sons-in-law, Lewis Ayres and Kent Allen.

Rachel, Hopewell, will Aug. 21, 1819; proved Sept. 17, 1819. Children, Christiana, Thomas S., Samuel B., Martha Ann, Sarah, and Hannah Andrews. Grandson, Samuel Andrews.

ERECKSON

John, Sr., Maurice River, will Mar. 1, 1802; proved Nov. 27, 1804. Wife, Louisa. Children, John, Silsbee, Jonathan, Mary, Hannah, Thomas, Hollingshead and Louisa.

ERICKSON

Thomas, Leesburgh, will Oct. 7, 1844; proved Nov. 18, 1844. Wife, Ann. Children, Mary Ann, William and John.

ERRICKSON

Andrew, Sr., Morris River, will Jan. 31, 1747; proved May 24, 1748. Wife, Modlena. Children, Andrew, Samuel, Christiana P. terson, Sarah Huings and Rebecca.

EVERINGHAM

Alfred F., Bridgeton, will Sept. 21, 1847; proved May 7, 1856. Wife, Prudence.

EWING

Enos, Greenwich, will July 1, 1834; proved Aug. 21, 1834. Wife, Rachel. Children, Mary, wife of Charles B. Fithian, and Sarah F., wife of Ephraim Bacon. Grandchildren, Enos E., Charles and Mary Fithian, and Enos E., son of Ephraim and Sarah Bacon.

Joshua, will July 31, 1784; proved Aug. 15, 1785. Children, Palmis, Joshua, James, Robert, Elizabeth and Anna. Brothers, Maskell, James and John Ewing.

Mary, will Feb. 14, 1781; proved Mar. 29, 1785. Children, Masell, Thomas, Phebe, Mary Diament, John, Samuel and Joshua. Granddaughter, Palmis, daughter of Joshua. Daughters-in-law, Martha, wife of Thomas, and Mary, wife of Samuel.

Maskell, Greenwich, Mar. 30, 1790; proved Apr. 18, 1796. Wife, Mary. Children, Abigail, Phebe, Amey, Mary, Sarah, Rachel, Snsauna, Maskell and David. Grandson, William B. Ewing.

Thomas, Sr., Cohansey, will Jan. 7, 1744/5; proved Apr. 7, 1748. Wife, Mary. Children, Maskell, John, Thomas, Mary, Joshua, Samuel, James.

Thomas, Greenwich, Nov. 2, 1767; proved June 15, 1771. Wife, Sarah. Children, Joel, George, Dixon, Rachel and Phebe. Brother, Maskell Ewing.

Thomas, Greenwich, Aug. 9, 1782; proved Feb. 21, 1783. Wife, Sarah. Son, William B. Brother, Maskell Ewing.

William, Cohansey, will Apr. 7, 1749; proved May 1, 1749. Brother, James Ewing. Brother-in-law, Charles Dennis, Jr.

FANVER

Joseph, Deerfield, will Apr. 6, 1804; proved Aug. 30, 1806. Wife, Ruth. Children, Ruth, Ann, Jacomintia Borton and Elizabeth Bishop. Daughter-in-law, Polly Swing.

FILER

John, Deerfield, will Nov. 18, 1775; proved Nov. 5, 1776. Wife, Sarah. Brothers, William, Robert and George Filer. Sister, Abigail Bateman. Nephews, John, son of Robert Filer, and John, son of George Filer.

Sarah (widow of John), will Apr. 2, 1781; proved June 1, 1786. No relationship shown.

FILLMAN

Henry, Greenwich, will Dec. 6, 1856; proved Aug. 8, 1857. Wife, Margaret.

FINLAW

James, Stow Creek, will May 25, 1784; proved June 18, 1784. Children, Low, James, Mary, Amy and Rebeckah. Brother, John. Nephew, William, son of John Finlaw.

John, Stow Creek, will Mar. 20, 1757; proved June 17, 1757. Wife, Rebeckah. Children, James, David, William, Margaret Long, John, Nathan, Elizabeth, Jane and Sarah.

FISH

Asa, Cedarville, will Feb. 12, 1838; proved Aug. 29, 1859. Wife mentioned, but not by name. Children, Nathaniel; others mentioned, but not by name.

Hannah, Deerfield, will Nov. 6, 1783; proved Nov. 29, 1783.

Children, Susannah, Jonathan and Sarah. Brothers, David and Rinear Dare.

FISHER

Elizabeth, Bridgeton, will Mar. 10 1853; proved May 17, 1854 Children, Rachel Haines, Joseph, John and William Fisher.

FISLER

Benjamin, Maurice River, will Oct. 21, 1842; proved Aug. 25, 1854. Children, Caroline, George F., Samuel, Jane, wife of Jacob Mulford, and Eliza (dec'd). Granddaughter, Emma D. Mulford.

FITHIAN

Aaron, will July 19, 1776; proved Jan. 7, 1777. Wife, Mary. Daughter, Ame.

Daniel, Fairfield, will Mar. 20, 1793; proved Apr. 29, 1793. Wife Rhodah. Children mentioned, but not by name.

David, Fairfield, will Feb. 15, 1754; proved Apr. 29, 1754. Wife, Temperance. Children, David, Ephraim, Levi, Lot, Jonathan, Aaron, Joseph, Temperance and Sarah.

David, will Apr. 27, 1816; proved June 3, 1816. Wife, Lydia. Children, George; others mentioned, but not by name.

David, Millville, will not dated; proved Nov. 20, 1852. Wife, Eunice. Children, James W. and Thomas S.

Enoch, Hopewell, will June 26, 1838; proved Oct. 3, 1842. Wife, Susannah. Daughter, Mary Ann Mulford.

Ephraim, Greenwich, will May 6, 1770; proved June 1, 1773. Wife, Temperance. Children, Matthias, Ira and Phebe. Cousin, Samuel Fithian.

George, Fairfield, will July 14, 1860; proved Aug. 25, 1860. Wife, Mary. Daughter, Emily.

Glover, will May 17, 1806; proved May 24, 1806. Wife, Prudence. Children, Sarah, Isaac, David and Benjamin. Brother, Isaac, Fithian.

GENEALOGICAL DATA

Isaac, Bridgeton, Feb. 17, 1810; proved Apr. 27, 1810, Wife, Sarah. Sister, Elizabeth, wife of Benjamin Maul. Grandson, Isaac Fithian, son of William Gilman. Stepson, William Gilman.

Joel, Roadstown, will May 27, 1800; proved Nov. 23, 1821. Wife, Elizabeth. Children, Josiah, Charles, Enoch, Samuel (dec'd), and Philip. Grandchildren, Sarah D., daughter of Samuel Fithian, and Mary Elizabeth, daughter of Erkuries Fithian.

Joel, Hopewell, will Sept. 21, 1839; proved Dec. 28, 1839. Wife, Hannah A. Children of second wife, Jonathan, Lydia W., Elizabeth and Joel.

John, Bridge Town. July 2, 1788; proved Mar. 21, 1789. Children, Lot, John, Isaac, Unis, Elizabeth, William, Ezekiel and Thomas. Sister, Molly Wheaton.

John, Hopewell, will Jan. 31, 1813; proved Feb. 8, 1813. Wife, Phebe. Brothers, Jonathan, Enoch and Moses Fithian.

Jonathan, will Aug. 21, 1791; proved Sept. 17, 1791. Wife, mentioned, but not by name. Daughter, Rebeckah. Brother Lot Fithian.

Josiah, Greenwich, will Nov. 22, 1766; proved Dec. 27, 1766. Wife, Ann. Brothers, Joseph and Samuel Fithian.

Josiah, Greenwich, will not dated; proved Apr. 12, 1777. Brothers, Jonathan and Amos.

Martha, Greenwich, will Jan. 24, 1779; proved Feb. 2, 1779. Children, Silvester, and Esther Maskell. Grandchildren, Sally and Abijah Maskell and Enoch Mulford.

Matthias, will May 29, 1749; proved Oct. 24, 1749. Children, Humphrey, Daniel, William, Ephraim; five others mentioned, but not by name.

Nathan, Deerfield, will June 21, 1831; proved Feb. 2, 1832. Wife Mary. Children, Joel and Sarah. Father, William Fithian (dec'd).

Philip V., Hopewell, will July 2, 1776; proved Apr. 12, 1777. Wife, Elizabeth. Brothers, Amos, Thomas and Josiah.

FROM CUMBERLAND COUNTY WILLS 53

Reuben, will not dated; proved Apr. 9, 1853. Brothers, John B., Joel and Robert. Sister, Ruth Fithian.

Samuel, Greenwich, will May 10, 1751; proved Apr. 6, 1752. Wife, Abigail. Brothers, Isaac and Josiah. Cousins, Lot, Samuel and John Fithian.

Samuel, Hopewell, Jan. 21, 1776; proved May 5, 1778. Children, Joel. Seeley, Samuel, Mary, Sarah, Ruth, Hannah Leake, Rachel Clark, Amy Moore and Elizabeth.

Samuel C., Greenwich, will May 14, 1859; proved May 30, 1859. Wife, Rebecca. Children, Harriet N. Miller. Cornelia Margaret and Josiah F. Son-in-law, Charles Miller.

FLANAGAN

James, will Apr. 30, 1860; proved Dec. 1860. Children, Rachel Glaspey, James H., Harris, Elizabeth S. Dare, Mary Ann Mulford, Jacob, John and Hannah N.

FOSTER

Ezekiel, Deerfield, will Feb. 24, 1787; proved May 14, 1788. Children, Ezekiel, Jeremiah, Patience, Martha and Elisheba.

Hannah, Deerfield, will Sept. 29, 1818; proved Dec. 16, 1818 Children, Ephraim, Nathaniel; Jeremiah, Sarah DuBois, Phebe Sneathen, Ruth Thompson, Hannah McQuean, Elizabeth Newkirk and Esther Foster.

Jeremiah, Deerfield, will Feb. 11, 1772; proved Feb. 27, 1787. Children, Ezekiel, Ephraim, Patience James, Jonathan, Phebe Rose, Sarah Bacon, Esther Stratton, Temperance Ogden, Abigail Titas and Amey Boyd.

Nathaniel, will Feb. 25, 1857; proved Apr. 18, 1860. Children, Mary Ann, wife of James Hutton, Nathaniel, Louisa Blackson, Ruth Colvin and Hannah Wilkinson. Granddaughter, Angelina Hutton.

FOX

Charles, wlll Jan. 31, 1756; proved Mar. 20, 1758. Wife, Mary

Children, William, James, John, Mary, Esther, Gatte, Ephraim and Charles.

William, Dividing Creek, will Feb. 19, 1760; proved Mar. 31 1760. Wife, Deborah.

FRARY

Spencer, Fairfield, Mar. 24, 1851; proved June 25, 1852. Wife, Abigail. Sons, Horace and Hiram.

FRAZER

Hannah, Fairfield, will May 7, 1760; proved Oct. 28, 1760. Brother, Seth Lore. Sisters, Ann Dollas, Phebe Lore and Abigail Westcot. Cousins, Ann Lore, Hannah Eldreg, Elizabeth Dollas, and Hannah, daughter of Abigail Westcot.

FRAZIER

Richard, Deerfield, will not dated; proved May 25, 1855. Wife, Ann.

FRAZURE

Caleb, Deerfield, will Feb. 5, 1851; proved May 23, 1851. Wife, Ann. Seven children mentioned, but not by name.

Samuel, Cohansey, Feb. 2, 1860; proved Mar. 18, 1860. Wife, Susan. Children mentioned, but not by name.

FRENCH

Deborah, Downe, will Apr. 20, 1858; proved Oct. 11, 1858. Children, William, Ephraim, Nathaniel and Jonathan Lore.

FULLER

James, Bridgeton, will Jan. 26, 1848; proved Feb. 14, 1848. Wife, Ruth. Children, Emeline, Jane and Harriet.

FURNES

Margaret, Maurice River, will Nov. 9, 1809; proved June 7, 1810. Children, Samuel and Mary

FURNISS

William, Maurice River, will Jan. 1, 1792; proved Feb. 17, 1792. Wife, Margaret. Children, Samuel, Mary VanHook and Edith Neidy.

FURROW

Felix, Stow Creek, will Aug. 30, 1791; proved Oct. 11, 1791. Wife, Elizabeth. Children, Bershabe Goodrat, Susannah Murphy and Mary, wife of Thomas Lasley.

GAIL

Samuel, Maurice River, will Dec. 26, 1805; proved Jan. 18, 1806. Wife mentioned, but not by name. Sons, David and George.

GANDY

Aaron, Fairfield, will Jan. 24, 1772; proved Mar. 10, 1773. Wife, Elizabeth Children, Abijah, Moses, Elishaba Huit and Hannah.

Abijah, will Apr. 23, 1776; proved Mar. 12, 1777. Wife, Mary. Children, Abijah, Shepherd and Deborah.

David, Downe, will Nov. 13, 1772; proved Aug. 17, 1775. Children Thomas, David and Ephraim; three youngest children mentioned, but not by name.

Lovisa, Fairfield, will May 29, 1823; proved Mar. 12, 1825. Children, Nathan and Lovisa F. Grandson, John, son of Henry Powell.

Moses, will Dec. 26, 1776; proved Mar. 12, 1777. Brother, Abijah. Sisters, Elishabe Hewet and Hannah. Nephews and neice, Henry, Abijah and Shepherd, sons of brother Abijah, and Mary, daughter of Elishabe Hewet.

Thomas, will May 21, 1748; proved Aug. 31, 1748. Children, Aaron, David, Patience, Catherine, Sarah, Mary, Phebe, Hannah, Priscilla and Rebecca. Son-in-law, Nathan Shaw.

Thomas, Downe, will Jan. 3, 1832; proved Jan. 18, 1832. Children, Abigail L., Ann, Thomas and George W. Son-in-law, John Lore.

GARRET

Susan H., Greenwich, will Sept. 13, 1854; proved Nov. 24, 1854. Brother, Thomas Garret. Sisters, Sarah, wife of Thomas McCollen, Elizabeth, wife of William Biddle, Margaret, wife of John Sheppard. Sister-in-law, Frances, wife of brother Thomas. Uncle, Edward Garret. Aunts, Margaret Marlin and Abigail S. Garret. Nephew and neice. Philip C. and Frances Garret.

GARRISON

Abraham, Deerfield, will Aug. 19, 1765; proved Oct. 22, 1766. Wife, Marcy. Children, Christian, wife of Joseph Chamlis, Rachel, wife of Hance Woolson, Isaac, Joseph, Samuel, Levi, Abraham, and Elizabeth, wife of Christopher Foster.

Abraham, Deerfield, will Feb. 27, 1775; proved Mar. 4, 1775. Wife, Abigail. Daughter, Lydia.

Abraham R., Bridgeton, will Jan. 11, 1839; proved Mar. 13, 1839. Wife, Mary.

Benjamin, will Aug. 28, 1767; proved Dec. 13, 1782. Children, David, Annanias, Mathias, Abigail, Susannah, Miriam Preston and Jonathan.

Charles, Millville, will Oct. 20, 1841; proved May 29, 1843. Brother Lewis Garrison. Neice, Mary, daughter of Lewis Garrison. Grandfather, Benjamin Garrison. Adopted son, Charles G., son of Daniel and Lydia Ireland. Wife's brothers, Lewis and Samuel.

Charles O., Hopewell, will Feb. 2, 1858; proved Oct. 11, 1858. Wife, Martha. Children mentioned, but not by name.

Daniel, Deerfield, will Dec. 4, 1799; proved Jan. 11, 1800. Wife, Phebe. Children, David, Ezekiel, Sarah Fithian, Rachel Still, Ann, Elizabeth Hoover, Phebe Black and Abigail Sailor. Grandson, Eli Garrison.

David, Deerfield, will Apr. 10, 1790; proved Sept. 30, 1790. Wife, Mary. Children, Joel, Mary Paris, Elizabeth, David O., Josiah and Azel.

David O., Deerfield, will June 7, 1850; proved Oct. 26, 1850. Wife, Sarah. Children, Elizabeth, Daniel D., Charles O. and David F.

Isaac, Deerfield, will May 12, 1767; proved July 11, 1767. Wife, Hannah. Children, Mary Covoing, Hannah Gagers, Ester, Abraham, Rumey, Catren, Bennit, Joseph, Jeremiah, Syles and Alfeas.

Isaac, Turkey Point, will May 2, 1784; proved Feb. 20, 1795. Wife, Rachel. Children, Henery, Rachel Glassby, Unice Lake, Abrrham and Jeremiah.

Isaac, Newport, will Nov. 16, 1819; proved Feb. 16, 1820. Wife, Nancy. First wife, Naomi.

Jacob, Deerfield, will July 15, 1750; proved Apr. 30, 1751. Wife, Elizabeth. Children, Benjamin, Christian Josling, Rachel Platts, Samuel, Sarah Reves, Jacob, Mary Stevens, Elizabeth, Daniel, Ephraim, William, Cornelius, Anna, Phebe and Alphais.

Jacob, Fairfield, will Nov. 17, 1766; proved Jan. 11, 1774. Children, Cornelas, John, Dabbora and Jarusha.

Jeremiah, Deerfield, will May 30, 1783; proved Mar. 20. 1786. Children, William, Elizabeth, Phebe Thompson, Jemima Smith and Rachel Maul.

John, Downe, will Sept. 3, 1776; proved June 18, 1777. Wife, Rebeka. Children, Sary, Nancy, Prudence, Jean and Elener. Brother, Henry, who has sons Isaac and Henry.

John, will Feb. 3, 1783; proved May 13, 1783. Wife, Jemima. Sons, Abraham and William. Grandchildren, Moses, son of Abraham, Jonathan and Tamson Garrison.

Jonathan T., Stoe Creek, will Apr. 18, 1847; proved July 23, 1847. Wife, Hannah. Children, Ann Dunham (dec'd), John, Abigail, William, and Sarah, wife of Ephraim P. Ayres. Grandsons, Abijah and William, sons of John Garrison.

Mary, Deerfield, will Oct. 9, 1805; proved Nov. 4, 1805. Children, Charles, whose wife is Lydia, and Samuel. Neice, Mary, daughter of brother Levi Leake.

Powell, Fairfield, will June 29, 1836; proved Jan. 8, 1838. Wife, Sarah. Children, Sarah Ogden and Powell H.

Ruth (widow of William), Deerfield, will Apr. 16, 1823; proved Apr. 19, 1823. Children, Edmund F., George W., Amos F. and Charles. Sister-in-law, Hannah Leake. Daughter-in-law, Hannah Garrison. Late husband's daughter, Ruth Leake.

Samuel, Deerfield, will Dec. 31, 1806; proved Aug. 17, 1807. Wife, Sarah.

Sarah Ann, will not dated; proved May 23, 1855. Children, Elizabeth and Daniel. Granddaughter, Meriah Ogden Jones.

Stephen, Millville, will Mar. 8, 1828; proved Oct. 23, 1828. Children, Hannah, wife of James Garrison, Rachel, wife of John Wright, Sarah, wife of Daniel Loper, Ann, Ruth, wife of William Porch, Susanna; Samuel and Stephen. Grandsons, William, Samuel and John, sons of daughter Ann.

William, Deerfield, will Jan. 21, 1817; proved May 22, 1819. Wife, Ruth. Children, Ruth Leake, Abijah, Charles, Edmund F., George W,, Amos F. and William G.

GARTON

Jonathan, Deerfield, will Apr. 20, 1824; proved Nov. 29, 1824. Wife, Anna. Children, Mark, Jonathan, David, Ephraim, Aaron James, Joseph and Levi. Granddaughter, Ann, daughter of Mark Garton.

GASKILL

Benjamin, Downe, will May 29, 1840; proved July 30, 1840. Wife, Esther. Children mentioned, but not by name. Brother Abel Gaskill.

Esther, Downe, will Jan. 18, 1845; proved Mar. 7, 1845. Children, Esther, Zerobable, Charles, Stephen and Benjamin Franklin Gaskill.

GENTRY

John, Deerfield, will Jan. 4, 1785; proved May 5, 1785. Wife, Hannah. Children, William, Thomas, Bateman, Susanna, Hannah, Ruth, Orpha, Sarah and Unice.

GIBBON

John, Stow Creek, will Dec. 10, 1776; inventory Oct. 9, 1778. Wife, Esther. Children, Hannah, Rachel, Nicholas, Ephraim, Leonard and Edmond.

Leonard, will Dec. 28, 1767; proved Jan. 27, 1768. Wife, Mary. Children, Mason, Rebecca and Martha. Brother, John Gibbon.

GILES

James, Bridgeton, will Mar. 8, 1823; proved July 30, 1825. Wife, Hannah. Children, Maria, wife of Abraham H. Inskeep, Fannie, wife of Isaac W. Hampton, and Nancy wife of Charles Read

GILMAN

Abraham, Hopewell, will May 5, 1792; proved Sept. 1, 1792. Wife, Sarah. Son, William. Father-in-law, Thomas Sheppard.

Daniel, Stow Creek, will Feb. 21, 1842; proved Nov. 23, 1843. Wife, Mary. Children, Ambrose, Elizabeth, Daniel, Abel, Keturah Brooks, John, William C., and Sarah Kinly.

David, Stow Creek, will June, 1783; proved Jan. 4, 1795. Children David, Elenor Dare and Letitia Platts.

David, Stow Creek, will Mar. 20, 1810; proved Apr. 30, 1810. Wife, Lydia. Children, Daniel, Uriah, Hannah, Ann, Lydia, Sarah and Letitia.

Uriah, Stoe Creek, will Dec. 18, 1848; proved Sept. 1, 1851. Wife, Mary. Children, Lemuel, Stratton, Abraham R., Elizabeth White, Benjamin and Ephraim.

William, Stoe Creek, will July 3, 1848; proved July 28, 1848. Wife, Rachel. Children, David H., Ellen W., Hannah E., Rachel S. Brooks and Letisha C. Robinson.

GITHENS

Samuel, Greenwich, will Apr. 20, 1846; proved Jan. 3, 1847. Children, William (dec'd), Joseph (dec'd), Hannah, wife of Samuel Mulford. Grandchildren, Alvira, Josephine, Mary and

William Lewis, children of William Githens, and Samuel, son of Joseph Githens. Brother George Githens, has a daughter Sarah.

GLAN

Gabriel, Downe, will Nov. 15, 1796; proved Oct. 19, 1798. Wife, Pheabe. Children, Frazar, Ruth Heaton, Anne, Sarah, Hannah, Elizabeth, Rhoda, Lovisa, Catharine, and an expected child.

GLANN

Ann, Downe, will Dec. 8, 1837; proved Apr. 12, 1852. Sisters, Elizabeth Pasley, Rhoda Busby, Ann Mayhew and Catharine Mayhew.

Levi, Downe, will Nov. 7 1856; proved Jan. 8, 1857. Brothers, Gabriel, Frazier and Daniel. Sisters, Rachel, Ruth, Mary L., Hannah, wife of Uriah Lore, Rebecca, wife of Jonathan Lore, and Sarah, wife of James Smith.

GODFREY

James, Maurice River, will Apr. 22, 1834; proved Apr. 25, 1835. Wife, Abigail. Children, Roxanna Ingersoll, Rachel Reeves, Ann Still, Sarah Errickson, James, Andrew, and Abigail Budd.

GOFF

Jeremiah, Maurice River, will July 12, 1761; proved Aug. 25 1761. Wife, Asenath. Children, Joseph, Jeremiah, Nathan, Mary and Hannah.

Joseph, Downe, will Feb. 25, 1777; proved June 17, 1777. Wife, Priscilla. Brothers, John, Jeremiah and Nathan. Sister, Hannah Goff. Brother-in-law, John Causon.

GOLDEN

Alpheus, Hopewell, will May 4, 1791; proved May 30, 1791. Wife, Lydia. Daughter, Clarissa. Brothers, Joseph and David. Sisters, Elizabeth Golden and Lodemah Keen.

Elizabeth, Bridgeton, will Mar. 9, 1826; proved Mar. 28, 1826

Brother, Joseph Golden. Sister, Lodemia. Neice, Ann McGilliard, daughter of sister Lodemia.

Joanna, Bridgeton, will Mar. 19, 1816; proved May 11, 1816. Children, Lodema McGilliard and Joseph.

John, Hopewell, will Dec. 2, 1789; proved Dec. 28, 1789. Wife, Joanna. Children, Alpheus, Joseph, David, Elizabeth, Lodema and Joanna. Son-in-law, Benjamin Keen,

Joseph, Bridgeton, will Sept. 11, 1854; proved Oct. 7, 1854. Wife, Ruth.

GOLDIN

John, Maurice River, will Mar. 13, 1765; proved Dec. 20, 1766. Wife, Rebecca. Children, Sary Garrison, Mary Smith, Judith, Hannah, Rebecca, Catherine, Rachel and Jean.

GOOLD

Benjamin, Fairfield, will May 9, 1777; proved June 16, 1777. Wife, Ann. Children, Sarah, Anthony, Samuel, Abijah and Elisha.

GOULD

Anthony, will June 23, 1803; proved Sept. 27, 1803. Children, Phebe, Christon and Mathela.

Jesse, Bridgeton, will Mar. 13, 1849; proved Mar. 29, 1849. Wife, Hannah. Children, Emily, Enoch, Freeman, Matilda and Hezekiah.

GOULDEN

Joseph, Deerfield, will Sept. 9, 1765; proved Oct. 23, 1765. Children, John, Joseph, Samuel, Sarah and Abilal.

GRACE

Phililip, Maurice River, will Nov. 13, 1826; proved Jan. 16, 1827. Children, William, John, Dolly, Hannah, and Catharine, wife of George Fox. Grandson, Samuel Hollingshead, son of daughter Hannah.

GRADEN

Dorothy, Stow Creek, will Mar. 26, 1755; proved Apr. 3, 1755. Granddaughter, Lucy, daughter of Peter Daten.

GREEN

Enoch, Deerfield, Sept. 9, 1775; proved May 6, 1777. Wife, Mary. Children, William and Nancey.

GRIFFITH

Elizabeth, Cohansey, will June 3, 1853; proved Dec. 31, 1853. Brother, Genet Hewitt.

Jesse, Greenwich, will July 10, 1837; proved Mar. 18, 1845. Wife, Nancy.

Joseph, Hopewell, will Jan. 6, 1850; proved June 7, 1851. Wife, Elizabeth. Nephews, Abel G. and George P. Cheesman.

GRISCOM

Andrew, Stow Creek, will Jan. 22, 1761; proved June 9, 1773. Wife, Mary. Children, Mary, Deborah, Everett, William, Sarah and Andrew.

GROOM

Peter, Maurice River, will, Aug. 29, 1804; proved Jan. 29, 1807. Wife, Tabitha. Children, Peter, Christiana Robertson, Mary, Jenney and John.

Tabitha, Maurice River, will Oct. 20, 1825; proved Mar. 20, 1832. Children, Phebe, wife of David Mason, Prudence, wife of Joseph Doughty, and Jonathan Lore.

HALL

Aron, Bridgeton, will Jan. 22, 1844; proved Feb. 13, 1844. Wife, Lovica Ann. Sons, David and Henry.

Jacob, Hopewell, will Feb. 13, 1818; proved Mar. 23, 1818. Wife, Phebe. Daughter, Hannah Sheppard.

HAMMITT

Jacob, Greenwich, will Sept. 19, 1794; proved Feb. 4, 1805. Wife, Frances.

HAMPTON

John Thomas, Fairfield, Sept. 29, 1794; proved Aug. 18, 1794. Wife, Mercy. Children, John, William H., Isaac H., and James H.; daughters mentioned, but not by name.

HAND

Abraham, Fairfield, will May 11, 1759; proved June 21, 1759. Wife, Hannah. Father, Benjamin Chard.

Nathan, Maurice River, will Nov. 24, 1805; proved Dec. 14, 1805. Adopted children mentioned.

Nathaniel, Hopewell, will Nov. 29, 1797; proved Dec. 9, 1797. Wife, Abigail. Children, Mary, Rachel, John, Noah, Thomas, Abijah and Abigail.

HANN

Jonathan, Bridgeton, will Feb. 12, 1826; proved Mar. 3, 1826. Wife Mary. Sister-in-law, Dolly Hann.

HANNAH

Bathsheba, Greenwich, will July 20, 1835; proved Mar. 23, 1840. Daughter, Martha Tomlinson. Granddaughter, Martha Pierson.

James, Deerfield, will Feb. 21, 1773; proved May 12, 1773. Wife, Ruth. Son, David. Brother, Preston Hannah. Mother, Lydia Hannah.

Michael, Deerfield, will Sept. 14, 1752; proved Oct. 6, 1753. Wife mentioned, but not by name. Children, Meriam, Mary, Sarah and Samuel.

Samuel, Deerfield, will Mar. 8, 1769; proved Nov. 8, 1770. Wife, Lida. Children, Abigail, Silas, Mary, James and Preston. Father, Michael Hannah.

HANNAN

Adam, Deerfield, will Apr. 7, 1835; proved Dec. 2, 1837. Children, George, Christiana Ott, Sarah Hitchner, Susannah Coombs (dec'd), and Margaret. Grandchildren, Mary, daughter of John Hannan, George, son of George Hannon and Adam, son of son-in-law, Mathias Hitchner.

HANNER

Ann. Greenwich, will Jan. 28, 1831; proved Mar. 3, 1831. Mother, Mary, wife of William White. Children, Mark, Sarah, Elwood, Richard, Ruth and Letitia. Father-in-law, William White.

Charles B., Greenwich, will Jan. 22, 1828; proved Mar. 12, 1828. Wife, Mary T. Brother, Josiah Hanner.

HANNON

John Filer, Deerfield, will Aug. 28, 1855; proved Dec. 31, 1855. Brother, George F. Hannon.

HANTHORN

Isaac, Deerfield, will Jan. 4, 1820; proved Nov. 11, 1837. Children, Charles, John, Sarah, Mary, Richard, Nancy, Elizabeth and George.

John, Bridgeton, will Sept. 2, 1858; proved Aug. 16, 1859. Children, Simon, Daniel, John and Enoch.

HARDING

Jeremiah, Greenwich, will Apr. 1, 1788; proved May 14, 1788. Wife, Dorothy. Children, Isaac, John, Hannah, Richard, Samuel and Sarah.

John, Greenwich, will Apr. 30, 1841; proved Sept. 21, 1841. Children, Benjamin, John B., Priscilla, wife of James Williams, Martha, wife of James I. Ewing, and Hannah Ann, wife of Erkuries Fithian.

HARMER

Joseph, Greenwich, will Apr. 4, 1814; proved May 5, 1814. Wife, Letitia. Children, Charles, Joseph, Ebenezer, Josiah, William and Rebecca.

Josiah, Greenwich, will May 24, 1847; proved Jan. 12, 1850. Wife, Hannah Ann. Children, Mary Ann, Lydia, Hannah Ann and Rebecca.

HARRIS

Abijah, Bridgeton, will June 24, 1841; proved July 18, 1848. Wife, Hannah. Children, Samuel, James E., Joseph, Charlotte Smith, Anna Maria Smith and Rachel.

Benjamin, Hopewell, will Nov. 14, 1776; proved Sept. 11, 1777. Wife, Rachel. Children, Ogden, Benjamin, Johnson, Alva, Phebe, Ann, Priscilla and Rachel.

Daniel, Hopewell, will June 23, 1776; proved Aug. 1, 1776. Wife, Martha. Children, Robert, Daniel, Hosea, Joel, Amos, Eunice and Mary.

Daniel, will Aug. 26, 1844; proved June 13, 1846. Children, Philip, Rebecca Gilman, Vickers and Daniel. Granddaughter, Paiscilla H. Sheppard.

David, Fairfield, will Nov. 24, 1823; proved Nov. 26, 1823. Wife, Rhoda. Children, David, Ebenezer, Ephraim, John, James, Rhoda and Jonathan D. Children's grandmother, Sarah Diament.

Eleanor (widow of Johnson), Bridgeton, will Dec. 26, 1848; proved Mar. 7, 1853. Children, Charles, and Sarah, wife of Enoch Shoemaker. Grandchildren, Horace B. and Charles, children of Enoch and Sarah Shoemaker.

Ephraim, Fairfield, will Oct. 21, 1786; proved Dec. 27, 1794. Wife, Regine. Children, Ephraim, Thomas, John, Pierson, Jane Westcott and Hannah.

Ephraim, Fairfield, will Feb. 8, 1805; proved Mar. 19, 1805. Wife, Sarah. Children, Allen, John, Caty Smith and Harvey. Grandchildren, Ephraim H., son of Caty Smith, and Hannah S. Blackman. Father, Ephraim Harris.

GENEALOGICAL DATA

Ephraim, Fairfield, will Aug. 8, 1855; proved Sept. 9, 1856. Wife, Abigail. Children, Hannah O. Clever, Ephraim E. and David. Son-in-law, Lewis W. Tomlinson.

George, Downe, June 14, 1822; proved Nov 22, 1825. Wife, Mary. Children, Joseph, Mary and William.

Isaac, Cedarville, will Jan. 1, 1845; proved Apr. 3, 1849. Wife, Hannah L.

Jacob, Hopewell, Feb. 4, 1798; proved Mar. 31, 1798 Wife, Rachel. Children, Jacob, Hannah, Mary, Rachel, Merab and George. Father, Jacob Harris. Grandfather, Samuel Harris.

Jacob, Roadstown, May 2, 1854; proved Aug. 18, 1855. Wife Phebe. Children, Joseph L., Hannah L. Hall, William B·, Phebe M. Haas, Sarah S., Margaret F. and Jacob. Son-in-law Edwin Haas. Mother-in-law, Phebe Mulford.

John, Hopewell, will Jan. 27. 1824; proved Jan. 29, 1830. Wife, Elizabeth. Children, Cynthia Lupton, Lydia Lupton and Alvah Harris. Brother, Noah Harris.

Josiah, Hopewell, will June 15, 1776; proved July 5, 1776. Wife mentioned, but not by name. Children, Enos, Israel, John, Hannah and Elizabeth.

Josiah, Deerfield, will Jan. 3 1833; proved Feb. 2, 1833. Wife, Hannah. Sons, Noah and Hosea. Grandson, Hosea Harris. Wife's sons, Samuel and Ebenezer Harris.

Josiah, Deerfield, will July 22, 1852; proved Aug. 19, 1852. Father, Noah Harris. Mother Phebe Harris. Brothers, Mark and Lawrence Harris.

Moses, Hopewell, will Jan. 25, 1819; proved Sept. 17, 1823· Children, Elizabeth, wife of Samuel Bacon, Rachel, widow of Uriah Parvin, Abigail, wife of Jonathan Cook, and Almeda, wife of Eden M. Seeley.

Nathaniel, Hopewell, will June 27, 1770; proved Nov. 14, 1775. Children, Nathaniel, John, Jonathan, Uriah, Josiah, David, Hannah Ewing, Ruth Whiticar, Abigail Alderman and Elizabeth Bowen. Grandsons, Ebenezer Harris, and David, son of David Harris.

Noah, Deerfield, will Jan. 1, 1787; proved Mar. 11, 1777. Wife, Mary. Children, Tamsen, Susannah, Noah, Hannah, Meriam, Mary, Phebe and Abigail.

Rachel (widow of Jacob), Hopewell, will June 8, 1808; proved Dec. 31, 1811. Children, Hannah, George, Jacob and Mary.

Samuel, Hopewell, will Jan. 4, 1773; proved Jan. 30, 1773. Wife, Rachel. Children, J Abraham, Benjamin, Silas, Jacob (dec'd), Daniel, and Hannah Tomson. Grandson, Jacob, son of Jacob Harris.

Samuel B., Hopewell, will Aug. 12, 1811; proved Sept. 10, 1811. Brothers, Charles Harris and Edward Welch.

Silas, Stoe Creek, will July 6, 1818; proved Sept. 30, 1820. Ghildren, James, Silas, Samuel, and Margaret, wife of Daniel Noble. Grandchildren, Andrew Harris, Mary Tullis and Margaret Noble.

Thomas, Fairfield, will Oct. 24, 1749; proved Dec. 20, 1749. Wife, Anna. Children, Thomas, Isaac (dec'd), Jeremiah, Sarah Ogden anc Caleb. Grandchildren, Isaac, Thomas, Anna, Mercy, Mary, and Esther, children of son Isaac.

Thomas, will Feb. 6, 1781; proved March 17, 1784. Wife Susanna. Children, Ephraim, James, Amariah, Judith, Ruth Bower, Sarah Clark, Abigail Stratton and Barsheca Brooks. Father, Thomas Harris. Grandchildren, Isarc, Rutd, Sarah, Abigail and Barsheba Harris. Daughter-in-law, Ruth Lawrence.

Thomas, Fairfield, will Oct. 24, 1820; proved Mar. 15, 1825. Wife, Elizabeth. Children, Sarah E., Newton and Theophilus E.

Thomas, Stoe Creek, will Jan. 5, 1839; proved Feb. 6, 1839. Wife, Nancy. Children mentioned, but not by name.

HARWOOD

Rachel, Greenwich, will May 10, 1816; proved June 1, 1816. No relationshiy shown.

HAWKINS

Joseph, Hopewell, will Apr. 7, 1856; proved Feb. 2, 1857. Wife, Mary. Children, William, Caroline and Jane.

Peter, Fairfield, will Oct. 8, 1767; proved Jan. 26, 1768. Wife, Elizabeth. An expected child.

HAYS

John, Maurice River, will Apr. 19, 1845; proved June 8, 1852. Wife, Rachel, Children, Lewis, John, Daniel, William, Abia, Berthena, Elizabeth and Chrisiianna.

HEATON

Daniel, Downe, will not dated; proved Dec. 22, 1840. Wife, Ruth. Children, Anna Burt, Ruth Haley, and Gideon Heaton.

Gideon, Down, Mar. 28, 1788; proved Sept. 22, 1788. Wife, Anna. Children, Samuel, Daniel, Gideon and Anna.

Samuel, Downe, will Sept. 16, 1777; proved Dec. 25, 1777. Children, Ephraim, Levi, Sally, Abigail, Gideon, Thomas and Elioenai. Grandchildren, Levi and Samuel.

Samuel, Downe, will Dec. 12, 1789; proved Sept. 30, 1790. Wife, Mary. Children, Aula and Seth.

HENDERSON

Alexander, Maurice River, will Aug. 16, 1856; proved Oct. 1, 1856. Wife, Jane. Son, Alexander.

Joseph, Maurice River, will June 25, 1849. Wife, Judith. Children mentioned, but not by name. Mother, Mary Henderson.

Mary, will Feb. 21, 1856; proved May 5, 1856. Daughter, Priscilla Carlisle. Daughter-in-law, Judith Henderson.

HENSON

Nimrod, Deerfield, will April 11, 1837; proved May 7, 1846. Wife, Ruth.

HESS

John, Maurice River, will Mar. 6, 1820; proved June 6, 1821. Wife, Sylvenia. Children, Daniel, John, Thomas, Jonathan, George, Frederick, Samuel, Jonas, Elizabeth Vanaman, Margaret

Katts, and David. Grandsons, Elmer and John, sons of George Hess, and John, son of Margaret Katts.

Silvenia, Maurice River, will Mar. 13, 1845; proved Jan. 1, 1851. Cousin, Maria, wife of Isaac Smith.

HEUSTED

Mary, Stow Creek, will Dec. Dec. 25, 1834; proved Feb. 16, 1835. Daughter, Rhoda Wright.

HICHNER

Jacob, Stow Creek, will Apr. 19, 1789; proved Dec. 1, 1800. Wife, Mary Magdalene. Children, Juliana, Salome Rocap, Catharina Rammel, Mary Magdalena Sickle, Barbara Bacon, George, Mary Hepner, Andrew, Margaret May, and Martin.

HIGH

Joseph, Deerfield, will May 18, 1818; proved July 22, 1818. Wife, Sarah.

HININ

John Wildrick, Deerfield, will Aug. 1, 1780. Wife, Elizabeth. Sons, Adam and John.

HOFFMAN

John, Maurice River, will July 28, 1760; proved Sept. 3, 1760. Wife Elizabeth. Sons, Frederick, David and John. Brothers, Jonas and Frederick Hoffman.

Jonas, Maurice River, will Sept. 9, 1809; proved Apr. 6, 1810. Children, Jonas, William, Eli, Eleanor Swain, Pamele Wainwright, and Drusilla Ingersull. Son-in-law, Jonathan Swain. Grandchildren, James Hoffman; Christopher, son of Benjamin Baker; Mary Peterson, daughter of Jonathan Hoffman; Eleanor and Dorothy Hoffman.

HOGBIN

Abraham, will May 14, 1801; proved Aug. 8, 1801. Wife, Mary. Sons, Joseph and Amariah.

HOHENSCHILT—Hosiel

Adam, Stow Creek, will Aug. 21, 1754; proved Sept. 10, 1754. Children George, Justin, Michael, Adam Mary Welden, Christiana Ranshart, Louise and Mary. Grandchildren, Henry, George, Elizabeth and Mary Hosiel.

HOLLINSHEAD

George, Maurice River, will Dec. 19, 1755; proved Jan. 8, 1756. Wife, Anne. Children, James, Samuel, George, Mary Low, Grace Mosslander. Charity Crandol and Anne Regain. Father, William Hollinshead.

James, will Feb. 9, 1818; proved June 9, 1820. Daughter, Lovisa Duffee. Grandchildren, Polly Peterson (nee Huffman), Dorty Huffman, Hugh Fouller, William Fowler, Hollingshead Errickson. Fannie Errickson, Ann and Elizabeth Duffee.

HOLMES

Abijah, will Feb. 18, 1785; proved Oct. 11, 1785. Wife, Radhel. Children, Jonathan, John, Ephraim, Sarah and Mary.

Samuel, Greenwich, will Mar. 10, 1749/50; proved Mar. 28, 1750. Cousins, Jonathan Holmes and Obadiah Robbins.

HOPMAN

John, Maurice River, will Apr. 26, 1746; proved May 6, 1748. Wife, Cathren. Sons, John, Frederick, Peter, James and Gabriel. Neice, Mary Hopman.

HOSHEL

Michael, Stow Creek, will July 8, 1790; proved Apr. 4, 1795. Wife, Rachel. Grandchildren, Susanna, Hoshel and Samuel Scull. Nephew and neice, Michael and Polly Hoshel.

HOWELL

Ebenezer, Stow Creek, will Oct. 18, 1785; proved Dec. 7, 1787. Wife, Sarah. Children, Richard, Sarah Youngs and George. Grandson, Charles Howell.

FROM CUMBERLAND COUNTY WILLS   71

Edmund, Sayres Neck, will not dated; proved Mar. 18, 1860 Wife, Hannah. Children, Ruth, Cornelia, Anna, George, Orlando, Reuben, William, Henry, Benjamin and Martha E.

Elias, Fairfield, will Mar. 16, 1833; proved Mar. 25, 1834. Wife mentioned, but not by name. Children, Edmund and Martha.

George, will Sept. 19, 1845; proved Mar. 19, 1848. Children, Lewis, Charles, Ebenezer, Sarah and George. Grandchildren, Richard, Philip, Sarah F. and George Howell; George and Caroline children of son George (dec'd).

Hannah (widow of Elias), Fairfield, will June 15, 1841; proved Dec. 2, 1844. Children, Edmund and Martha. Granddaughters, Martha Elizabeth, daughter of Edmund, and Rosa, daughter of Martha.

Henry, Fairfield, will July 17, 1824; proved Nov. 20, 1824. Wife, Margaret P. Sons, Henry D. and John H. "Mother Westcott."

HUDSON

Obed, Greenwich, will Aug. 30, 1787; proved Nov. 10, 1787. Wife, Phebe. Children, Sally, Anna, Isaac and Joseph. Wife's Children, Richard and Sally Miller

HUNT

Bartholomew, Stow Creek, will Mar. 16, 1795; proved Sept. 20, 1796. Wife, Eleanor. Children, Elizabeth Johnston, Esther, James B., William and John (dec'd). Grandchildren, Richard and John, sons of John; and Margaret Johnston. Stepdaughter, Mary Currant.

Thomas E., Greenwich, will Oct. 7, 1858; proved Feb. 1, 1859. Children, Thomas E. and Mary C.

HUNTER

Andrew, Hopewell, May 10, 1774; proved Aug. 22, 1775. Wife, Amy. Brother, Nicholas Hunter. Sisters, Elizabeth Carr and Nancy Willock. Nephew and neices, Andrew Hunter and Rebecca and Elizabeth Carr.

HUSTED

Aaron, Fairfield, will Dec. 25, 1773; proved Feb. 23, 1774. Wife mentioned, but not by name. Son, Aaron. Brothers and sisters, Samuel, Moses, Elizabeth Powell, Mary Seeley and Ruhame Husted. Mother, Elizabeth Husted.

David, Fairfield, will Mar. 15, 1775; proved Apr. 6, 1775. Wife mentioned, but not by name. Children, David, Zephniah, Jeremiah, Jonathan, Hosea, Rhoda Burk and Joel.

Hosea, Fairfield, will May 22, 1823; proved June 2, 1823. Wife, Mary. Children, Ephraim, Hosea, John, Ruth Sutton and Rhoda.

Joel, Fairfield, will May 17, 1796; proved June 21, 1796. Wife, Mary. Children, Joel, William, David, Nancy and Polly.

Moses, Fairfield, will Aug. 23, 1773; proved Sept. 14, 1778. Wife mentioned, but not by name. Children, Samuel, Elizabeth, widow of Richard Powell, Mary, wife of Jesse Seeley, Ruhamah, Moses and Aaron.

Moses, Fairfield, will Feb. 25, 1788; proved Apr. 25, 1788. Wife, Content. Children, Moses, William, Joseph, Ruth, Elizabeth, Rachel, Anne and Abigail.

Peter, Deerfield, will May 23, 1858; proved July 28, 1858. Wife, Elizabeth. Children, Henry Mene Tasker and Frederick.

INDICUT

Barzilla, Maurice River, will Apr. 18, 1825; proved May 6, 1825. Children, Samuel, John, Thomas and Mary.

IRELAN

David, Hopewell, will Dec. 2, 1818; proved Dec. 11, 1818. Sisters, Phebe Bowen and Ann Woodruff. Nephew, Ananias Bowen.

Israel, Stoe Creek, will Nov. 27, 1831; proved Mar. 6, 1832. Wife, Elizabeth. Children, Rebecca, David, Joseph and Mary.

IRELAND

Daniel, Deerfield, will Apr. 28, 1852; proved June 14, 1852. Wife, Susannah.

Jacob, Hopewell, will Dec. 3, 1751; proved Jan. 3, 1752. Wife, Mary. Children, Jacob, Ananias, Silas and Isaac.

Job, Downe, will May 26, 1778; proved Jan. 30, 1784. Wife, Elizabeth. Children, Daniel, Joseph, John, Ruth Edwards, Elizabeth and Dorcas.

JAMES

Damon, Hopewell, will Oct. 17, 1774; proved Jan. 10, 1775. Children, David and Amy. Mother, Sarah Reeves.

Elenor, will Oct. 11, 1827; proved Jan. 28, 1829. Neice, Lydia James.

JARMAN

Reuben, Hopewell, will Oct. 2, 1776; proved Feb. 20, 1788. Wife, Ruth. Brother, Jonathan Jarman. Sister Susannah Ayers.

JELLY

Henry, Bridgeton, will Apr. 27, 1777; proved May 5, 1777. Wife, Mary.

JENKINS

David Hooper, will Mar. 26, 1775; proved July 29, 1778. Children, Daniel, Nathaniel, Thomas, Hannah Sheppard and Amy.

JESS

David, Fairfield, will Jan. 24, 1795; proved Jan. 27, 1797. Wife, Ann. Children, Thomas and Josiah; three daughters mentioned, but not by name.

JESSUP

Stephen, Deerfield, will Sept. 11, 1764; proved Nov. 17, 1764. Wife, Mary. Children, Daniel, John, Isaac, Sarah, and Abigail Davis.

JOHNSON

Barbara, will June 27, 1790; proved Oct. 25, 1794. Children, Daniel, John, David, George, Michael, Catharine Freese, Jacob, Samuel and Elizabeth.

James, Hopewell, will May 22, 1759; proved June 8, 1759. Wife, Eunice. Daughter, Mabel, wife of John Reeves. Grandchildren, Eunice and Joel Duvall and Johnson and Lemuel Reeves.

John, Greenwich, will Jan. 18, 1815; proved Feb. 21, 1815. Children, David, George, and Elizabeth Waddington.

Nahum, Stow Creek, will Sept. 12, 1847; proved Oct. 11, 1847. Wife, Sarah. Son, Joseph F. Brother, Joseph Johnson.

Nathan Downe, will Apr. 20, 1784; proved Feb. 21, 1785. Wife, Victorina. Children, Nathan, Victorina and Rachel.

Nicholas, will Dec. 15, 1791; proved Feb. 15, 1794. Children, Rodah, Josiah, Nicholas, Enos and William. Granddaughters, Martha and Rachel Johnson.

Othniel, Hopewell, will Dec. 22, 1759; proved Feb. 26, 1760. Wife and children mentioned, but not by name. Brother, Samuel Fithian.

Susiana, Stoe Creek, will Apr. 28, 1854; proved Apr. 2, 1855. Daughters, Sarah E. and Amanda Johnson. Brothers, David, William and Isaac Elwell. Former husband, Gamaliel Padget.

JONHSTON

Enos, Bridgeton, will Sept. 21, 1801; proved Feb. 10, 1803. Wife, Elizabeth.

John, Millville, will not dated; proved July 31, 1840. Wife, Elizabeth. Children, Benjamin; others mentioned, but not by name.

JONES

Abraham, Maurice River, will Dec. 15, 1785; proved Feb. 30, 1786. Wife, Jane. Children, Thomas, Abraham, Rebecca Shropshire, Elizabeth Peterson and Jane Stillwell.

Jonathan, Maurice River, will Sept. 1, 1831; proved Jan. 4, 1832. Wife, Mary. Children, William, Jesse, Sarah Baner and Owen Grandchildren, Hannah and Owen, children of Jesse; Anna and William Clothier; and Mary, daughter of William.

Thomas, Greenwich, will Apr. 10, 1823; proved June 28, 1823. Nephews and neices, Hannah Wilmer, Sarah Heaton; Charles, Richard, Horatio Anne and Hannah, children of Elizabeth Wood.

JOSLEN

Jacob, Deerfield, will Nov. 12, 1796; proved June 29, 1797. Wife, Mary. Children, John, Jeremiah, Israel, William and Ephraim. Grandson, Josiah Joslen.

John, Deerfield, will Dec. 13, 1796; proved May 29, 1797. Wife, Pheby. Children, Jeremiah, Amy and Mary.

JOSLIN

Ephraim, Deerfield, will July 29, 1805; proved Sept. 19, 1805. Wife, Susanna. Son, Daniel. Brother, Israel Joslin.

Samuel, Deerfield, will June 23, 1813; proved June 18, 1814. Wife, Gaine. Son, Jedidiah. Grandson, Daniel Joslin.

Thomas, Deerfield, will May 10, 1794; proved June 14, 1794. Wife, Priscilla. Children, David and Rachel. Wife's neice, Rachel, daughter of James Bennet. Wife's grandson, Elijah, son of James Bennet. Grandchildren, Lucy, Elizabeth and Joseph Thomas Joslin, and Enos and William, son of John Woodruff.

KEEN

Elias, Greenwich, will June 17, 1847; proved Aug. 28, 1847. Wife, Almira. Sons, Elias B. and John.

John, Hopewell, will Dec. 3, 1781; proved Mar. 3, 1784. Wife, Rachel. Children, Jeremiah, John, Jacob, Hannah, Mary, Rachel, Sarah and Kateren.

KELLY—Kelley

William, Greenwich, will July 7, 1758; proved Oct. 5, 1758. Wife, Mary. Children, John, Elizabeth and Mary.

KELSAY

Robert, Stow Creek, will Mar. 23, 1789; proved June 5, 1790. Children, William, Robert, Joseph, David and Miriam Bowen. Grandson, Robert, son of Joseph.

KEMBLE

William, will July 15, 1799; proved Mar. 15, 1800. Wife, Ruth. Children, William, Manley, Isaiah G. and Samuel.

KER

Anna, Bridgeton, Nov. 11, 1811; proved June 6, 1812. Children, Hannah Caldwell, Elizabeth McCarty and Margaret Freeman.

KING

Levi, will Oct. 13, 1845; proved Nov. 10, 1845. Children, James B., Elizabeth, Sarah, wife of Daniel Moore, Levi, Keziah, wife of James Moore, Mary Forsman, Isabella Corson and Margaret.

KINKADE

Jane, Millville, Dec. 2, 1845; proved Jan. 9, 1846. Children, Mary Jane, wife of Jacob Beidman, Thomas, Ellen, wife of George Hoover, and Jason.

KIRBY

Stephen, Hopewell, will Mar. 10, 1781; proved Feb. 20, 1782. Wife, Margaret. Brother, Thomas Kirby.

LADOW

Charles, Cedarville, will June 13, 1849; proved Aug. 14, 1857 Wife, Ruth.

Peter, Downe, will Apr. 30, 1810; proved June 20, 1810. Children, Rebeckey Russe, Rossel and Peter.

Phebe, Downe, will not dated; proved Sept. 22, 1823. Children, Hannah Green, Unis Orr, Elizabeth Griggery, Mary Wollan, Abigail Douglas and David Heaton.

LANGLEY

John D., Bridgeton, will May 27, 1846; proved Sept. 28, 1846. Wife, Sarah C. Half-sister, Zipporah Jones.

LANING

John, Fairfield, will May 20, 1826; proved July 5, 1826. Children, George, John, Anna Wheaton and Rhoda Mulford.

LANNING

John, Bridgeton, will Nov. 25, 1850; proved Dec. 29, 1850. Wife, Judith. Children, Richard, David, Mary Ann and Phebe W.

LATNEY

John, will Dec. 19, 1807; proved Dec. 15, 1807. No relationship shown.

LAWRENCE

Annie (widow of Norton), Fairfield, will July 13, 1807; proved Sept. 24, 1807. Sisters Abigail Burch, Mary Lummis, Elizabeth Thompson and Almeda Lummis. Sons by late husband, Leonard and Lemuel Lawrence. Nephews and neices, Daniel Elmer, Rufus Ramsay Lummis, Daniel Elmer Burch, Elizabeth Lummis and Anne Elmer Thompson.

Daniel, Fairfield, will Mar. 7, 1787; proved Jan. 24, 1792. Wife Ruth.

Daniel, Bridgeton, will Jan. 28, 1848; proved Mar. 10, 1847. Wife, Sarah. Three children mentioned, but not by name.

Henry, Cedarville, will May 25, 1825; proved Dec. 29, 1859. Wife mentioned, but not by name.

Lemuel, Cedarville, will Dec. 25, 1840; proved Jan. 18, 1841. Children, Lummis L. and Holmes D.

Nathan, Fairfield, will Dec. 14, 1778; proved Jan. 27, 1779. Wife, Tamson. Sons mentioned, but not by name. Daughter, Sarah.

Nathan, Hopewell, will not dated; proved June 1, 1773. Wife,

Elizabeth. Children, Nathan, John, Henry, Zachariah, Violette Hosea, Rhoda and Daniel.

Zachariah, Bridgetown, will Aug. 8, 1798; proyed Sept. 15, 1798. Wife, Elizabeth. Children, Alexander, Sarah, Maria and Horatio. Sons-in-law, Archibald Campbell and Moses Thompson.

LEAKE

Elizabeth, Deerfield, will Mar. 5, 1830; proved Mar. 20, 1832. Neices, Ruth and Mary L. Warne. Nephew, John L. Avery.

Ephraim, will Mar. 9, 1826; proved Mar. 29, 1826. Wife, Jane. Neice, Jane Ann Stanger.

Hannah, will Sept. 19, 1822; proved Mar. 5, 1823. Nephews, Joseph Miller and Isaac Oliver and Recompence Whitaker.

Hannah, will Aug. 17, 1828; proved Nov. 12, 1824. Children, Nothan, Ephraim, and Rachel Fithian. Grandchildren, Phebe and Anna Leake, Edmund Garrison and Mary Cake.

Nathan, Deerfield, will Dec. 2), 1730; proved, 1791. Wife, Hannah. Children, David, Nathan, Ephraim, Amey, Phebe, Rachel, Ruth and Rebecca.

Recompence, will Jan. 3, 1799; proved Apr. 17, 1801. Wife, Elizabeth. Children, Elizabeth, and Jemima Avery. Grandson, Recrmpence Leake.

Samuel, Sept. 18, 1773; proved Feb. 0, 1782. Wife, Elizabeth. Children, Samuel, Levi, Aaron, and Mary Garrison.

LEE

John, Maurice River, will Nov. 26, 1840; proved Dec. 28, 1840. Wife, Jemimah. Children, John, Abel, Rebecca Cullen, Jemimah Hoffman, Edward, Thomat and Rhoda.

Lorenzo, Fairfield, will Julp 16, 1848; proved Aug. 18, 1848. Father-in-law, Henry Sheppard.

Rhoda, Maurice River, will May 29, 1856; proved May 11, 1858. Children, Benjamin F., Francis, Clement J., and Elizebeth Osterhout.

LEWIS

Abraham, Greenwich, will Sept. 27, 1813; proved June 7, 1814. Wife, Dinah. Children, Lydia, Jane, Josiah and Joseph.

LIPPINCOTT

Grace, Greenwich, will Sept. 8, 1836; proved Apr. 23, 1838. Daughter, Grace Ann (dec'd). Brother-in-law, George Lippincott.

LODER

Daniel, Millville, will Sept. 24, 1841; proved Oct. 6, 1841. Wife, Kesiah. Children, Martin, Lemuel, Jane and Daniel.

LONG

David, will May 14, 1769; proved Dec. 8, 1769. Wife, Lucy. Son, Peter. Uncle, Thomas Sayre.

Grace (widow of Peter), Stow Creek, will July 19, 1771; proved Dec. 21, 1775. Daughters Eleanor Shepherd and Pleasant Newcomb. Grandchildren, Uriah, son of Peter Long, and Lydia Gilman. Son-in-law, William Newcomb.

John, Hopewell, will May 3, 1764; proved June 11, 1764. Son David. Brother, David Long.

Joseph, Hopewell, will Apr. 14, 1759; proved Oct. 17, 1760. Children, David, John, Malachi, Ellioner and Elizabeth.

Malachi, Hopewell, will Jan. 24, 1791; proved Dec. 22, 1813. Wife, Dorcas.

Peter, Stoe Creek, will Aug. 25, 1754; proved Mar. 26, 1755. Wife, Grace. Children, Ansell, David, Nathan, Eleonor Shepard and Pleasant.

Silas, Maurice River, will Feb. 20, 1837; proved Oct. 10, 1838. Son, William (dec'd). Daughter-in-law, Alice (widow of William). Grandchildren, Lovisa, wife of John Frederick, Alexander, Ann, Kersey, William and John.

LOPER

James, Deerfield, will Dec. 14, 1791; proved June 4, 1792. Children, Arthur, Uriah, Lovisa Elwell, Phebe Carl and Mary Tully. Grandson, James Loper.

John, Millville, will Aug. 7, 1852; proved Aug. 28, 1852. Wife, Hannah. Son, Daniel.

LORD

Joseph, Maurice River, will Oct. 6, 1766; proved Feb. 25, 1767. Wife, Mary. Children, Nathaniel, Catharine Westcoate, Flowrandor Corson, George, Joseph, Absolom, Hannah and Mary.

LORE

Abigail, Downe, will Jan. 21, 1824; proved Apr. 14, 1824. Children, Lummis Lore and Harriet Lawrence. Sister Hannah Terry.

Daniel, Downe, will Dec. 29, 1786; proved Sept. 25, 1787. Wife, Eve. Children, Ethen, Lensey, Hannah, Rachel, Phebe.

David, Maurice River, will Oct. 10, 1798; proved Nov. 16, 1798. Wife, Tabitha. Children, Jonathan, John, Phebe, Prudence and Elizabeth.

David, Port Elizabeth, will July 8, 1853; proved July 25, 1853. Wife, Hannah. Children, Jonathan, Harvey, Charles and David.

Ephraim, will Jan 7, 1759; proved Mar. 1, 1759. Wife, Anna. Sons, John and Jonathan.

Ethan, Downe, will Dec., 1839; proved Apr. 20, 1847. Wife, Rhoda. Children, Richard, Ethan, Daniel, Hannah, William C., Lucy (dec'd), wife of Samuel Compton, Rhoda and Joseph.

Hezekiah, Maurice River, will Mar. 12, 1770; proved June 15, 1770. Wife, Deborah. Children, Jonathan; David, Sarah, Rebeckah and Elizabeth.

Ichabod, will June 13, 1769; proved July 26, 1769. Wife, Elizabeth. Children, Dolas, Hezekiah and Lewis. Father-inllaw, William Dollas.

Ichabod. Downe, will not dated; proved May 1, 1848. Children, Frazure, and Nancy Tullis.

Isaac Downe, will May 2, 1806; proved May 15, 1806. Wife, Mary. Children, Lydia, Anna and Elenor.

John, Maurice River, will Jan. 22, 1847; proved Mar. 5, 1847. Brothers, Franklin and Benjamin H. Sister, Sarah Ann Lore.

Jonathan, Downe, Mar. 16, 1788; proved March 24, 1788. Wife, Temperance. Children, Dan and David. Grandchildren, Jeremiah, Anna and John, children of David.

Jonathan, Downe, Mar. 31, 1810; proved May 19, 1810. Daughter, Deborah. Uncle, Isaac Brown.

Jonathan, Maurice River, will Aug. 9, 1849; proved Dec. 1, 1853. Wife, Sarah S. Children, Teresa Smith, Elizabeth Compton, Sarah Darmen, Ann Mariah Coombs, Jonathan and David. Grandchildren, Beulah and Amanda, daughters of Jonathan.

Richard, will July 2, 1787; proved July 24, 1787. No relationship shown.

William, Fairfield, will Feb. 7, 1772; proved May 26, 1772. Wife, Elener. Children, Rosil, Gidon and Elizabeth.

LOW

William, will June, June 1, 1792; proved July 6, 1792. Wife, Mary. Children, William, Robert, Hannah, John and Mary.

LUDLAM

Providence, Greenwich, will June 1, 1792; proved Aug. 27, 1792. Children, Jacob, Judith Wheaton, Rachel Sayres, Phebe Sheppard, Sally Watson, Priscilla S. and Lydia. Grandchildren, Sarah Remington, Ephraim and Reuben Ludlam, and Providence, son of Norton Ludlam.

LUMMIS

Ebenezer, will Oct. 14, 1801; proved Mar. 30, 1802. Wife, Lydia. Children, William, John, Ebenezer, Sarah, Daten and Susannah.

Edward, Deerfield, will Feb. 6, 1773; proved Feb. 28, 1776. Wife, Margaret. Children, Noah, Edward, Ephraim, Parsons, Margaret, Mary, Vashti, Esther and Lydia.

Edward, Deerfield, will Feb 17, 1823; proved Mar. 1, 1823. First wife deceased. Second wife, Patience. Children, Mary (dec'd), Edward, Edith Garrison, Elizabeth Brown and Jane Smith. Father, Edward Lummis.

Ephraim, Jr., will July 17, 1813; proved Aug. 17, 1813 Daughter, Harriet.

Ephraim, Deerfield, will Jan. 22, 1822; proved June 2, 1824. Wife mentioned, but not by name. Children, Ephraim, and Lovica Parvin. Granddaughter, Harriet Ogden.

John, Millville, will Feb. 6, 1809; proved Feb, 17, 1809. Wife, Margrite. Brothers and sisters, Dayton Lummis, Susannah Ray, Sarah Lummis and Ebenezer Lummis.

Manoah, will Mar. 1, 1799; proved Mar. 9, 1799. Wife, Mary. Children, David and Almeda.

Margaret, Bridgeton, will June 14, 1856; proved Sept. 17, 1860. No relationship shown.

Mary, Fairfield, will not dated; proved Nov. 10, 1824. Grandchildren, Rufus Ramsay Lummis, and Horace and Daniel Elmer.

Samuel, Cohansey, will Aug. 6, 1748; proved July 20, 1750. Wife, Deborah. Children, Samuel, David, Henry, and an expected child.

LUMMUS

Daniel, will June 1, 1764; proved Mar. 17, 1769. Wife, Judith. Children, Jonathan, Daniel, Ebenezer, Joseph, Catharine and Hannah. Sisters, Sarah and Tamson Lummis.

LUPTON

Benjamin, Cohansie, will Apr. 1, 1791; proved July 8, 1794, Son-in-law David Parvin and his wife, Rachel. Granddaughter, Rachel, daughter of David and Rachel Parvin.

Cornelius, will Feb. 2, 1853; proved July 12, 1858. Wife, Mary.

Daniel, will Nov. 20 1783; proved Aug. 29, 1796. Wife, Rebecca. Children, Benjamin, Daniel, Bitha and Sarah.

Nathan, Hopewell, Oct. 25, 1770; proved Sept. 25, 1771. Wife, Susannah. Children, John, Nathan, Amy Padget, Phebe, Rachel, Hannah and Rumah.

MACLAIN

James, Fairfield, will Feb. 11, 1813; proved Mar. 18, 1813. Children, Sarah, James, Elias, Thomas and Ryley.

MADDEN

George, Fairfield, will Jan. 27, 1817; proved Jan. 21, 1819. Wife, Flora. Children mentioned, but not by name.

MALL

Benjamin, Deerfield, will Aug. 7, 1790; proved Jan. 5, 1792. Wife, Rachel. Children, Ashbury and Lydia. Son-in-law, John Waithman.

Robert, Hopewell, will June 23, 1759; proved July 10, 1759. Daughter, Elanner Blew. Grandchildren, Elizabeth, Abijah and Seeley Blew. Son-in-law, George Blew.

MARSEILLES

Elizabeth, Deerfield, will Sept. 3, 1839; proved Apr. 28, 1854. Children, Hugh Marseilles and Hannah Daughty.

MARSHALL

Randal, Maurice River, will not dated; proved Oct. 8, 1841. Wife, Mary. Children, Mary R., wife of Ebenezer Seeley, Thomas C. and Randolph. Granddaughter, Ann M., wife of Franklin D. Edmunds.

Ruth, Port Elizabeth, will May 26, 1829; proved Sept. 2, 1829. Children, William, Matilda Bitters and Lydia McCully.

MANYOTT

Jonathan D., Hopewell, will Sept. 25, 1814; proved Feb. 24, 1815. Wife, Sarah. Children, John R., Reuben, Hannah, Margarett, Maria and Rebecca.

MASKELL

Esther, Greenwich, will Aug. 31, 1805; proved Oct. 19, 1805. Children, Sarah Smith, Abijah and Hannah. Granddaughter, Esther M. Smith. Son-in-law, Edward Smith.

Sarah, Stow Creek, will Mar. 2, 1815; proved Mar. 25, 1815. Sister, Sabra Peck.

MASON

William, Downe, Will Nov. 23, 1798; proved Apr. 9, 1804. Wife, Lydia. Children, David, William, Elizabeth Blizard, Tabitha Conrow and Sarah S.

MASSAY

Thomas, Fairfield, will Dec. 27, 1792; proved Jan. 28, 1793. Wife, Hannah. Children, Elizabeth, Thomas and Tamson.

MATTISON

Joseph, Greenwich, will Apr. 21, 1849; proved May 22, 1849. Children, Phebe Ann, Seeley, Sarah Ann wife of Benjamin Saxton, Elizabeth R., wife of Noah Hewitt, and Mary Garrison. Grandchildren, Hannah Ann, wife of William McWilliams, Phebe Lathbury, Joseph B. and Henry, children of Seeley Mattison.

MAUGER

Josiah, Stow Creek, will Apr. 7, 1813; proved Aug. 30, 1813. Wife, Rachel.

Rachel, Stoe Creek, will Dec. 25, 1823, proved Jan. 15, 1824. Son, Ashbury Maul. Grandchildren, Thomas Waithman and Rachel Moncrief. Great-grandchildren, Lydia Waithman, Ruth and Elizabeth McPherson, daughters of Rachel Moncrief.

MAUL

Benjamin, Hopewell, will Aug. 13, 1776; pproved Dec. 16, 1776. Children, John, Sarah, Hannah, Lyda, Rebecca, Abigail and Benjamin,

Benjamin, Hopewell, will Oct. 5, 1841; proved Oct. 23, 1851. Wife, Hannah.

Jeremiah, Deerfield, Mar. 30, 1787; proved Apr. 21, 1787. Wife, Rachel. Children, David, John G. and Jeremiah. Brothers, Benjamin, Robert, William and Elaxander.

McCONNELL

Michael, Stow Creek, will Dec. 4, 1819; proved Dec. 31, 1819. Wife, Hannah. Children mentioned, but not by name.

McGEE

Robert, Bridgeton, will Apr. 12, 1823; proved Oct. 23, 1823. Wife mentioned, but not by name. Children, Ephraim, John, Robert L., Martha, Phebe and Sarah.

McGILLIARD

James, Hopewell, will Mar. 17, 1835; proved Apr. 6, 1840. Son James. Grandson, Francis Elmer Clunn.

McGLAUGHLIN

George, Maurice River, will Oct. 7, 1780; proved Dec. 18, 1780. Wife, Elizabeth. Sister, Elizabeth McGlaughlin.

McKEAG

John, will not dated; proved Nov. 6, 1856. Wife, Anne. Wife's mother, Hannah Rogers.

McLAEN

Robert, Roadstown, will June 20, 1851; proved Oct. 12, 1857. Children, Nathaniel P., Mary Ann and James.

MEEK

William, Fairfield, will June 29, 1773; proved Jan. 6, 1774. Wife, Esther. Children, Rachel, Mary and James.

MICKEL

Daniel, Fairfield, will Aug. 3, 1795; proved 1795. Wife, Mary.

MICKLE

Rachel, Fairfield, will June 12. 1813; proved Aug. 28, 1813. Brother, Jeremiah Harris. Sisters, Elizabeth Bateman, Jane and Abigail Harris. Brother-in-law, Aaron Bateman.

MILLER

Ebenezer, Greenwich, will Feb. 3, 1774; proved June 1, 1774. Wife, Sarah. Children, Ebenezer, John, William, Mark, Sarah Davis, Rebeckah Hall and Josiah. Grandchildren, Andrew Miller, Joseph Hannan, and Letitia, daughter of John Miller.

Elizabeth, Greenwich. will Dec. 27, 1819; proved Apr. 12, 1826. Nephew and neices, William, Sarah Ann and Eliza, children of brother William Miller. Brother, Ebenezer Miller.

Isaac, Greenwich, will Jan. 8, 1806; proved Feb. 28, 1821. Wife, Mary.

Israel, Cohansey, will Sept. 23, 1818; proved Oct. 30, 1820. Children, Samuel, John, Lovise Leslie and Charlotte.

Jacob, Hopewell, will July 23, 1787; proved Sept. 24, 1787. Wife, Catharine. Children, Jacob, George, Michael, Andrew, John, Barbary and Margaret.

John, Cohansey, will Sept. 12, 1740; proved May 17, 1749. Wife, Susannah.

John, Hopewell, will Sept. 16, 1771; proved Apr. 1, 1772. Wife, Rachel. Children, William, John, Eunice, Rachel; Mary and Samuel E. Brother, Samuel Miller.

John, Greenwich, will Jan. 16, 1804; proved June 7, 1804. Children, Leatitia, wife of Josiah Johnson, Mary Brown, William, Isaac, John and Jacob.

John, Cohansey, will July 23, 1842; proved Aug. 13, 1843. Children, Caroline, Rachel, Thomas H., Harriet, Ann and Israel.

John, Greenwich, will Dec. 12, 1853; proved Oct. 27, 1858. Wife, Cornelia (dec'd). Wife's neice, Eliza M. Shute.

Joseph, Deerfield, will Apr. 30, 1827; proved Nov. 9, 1829. Children, John L., William, Joseph, Hannah Blew, Mary Ann, Matilda and Rachel.

Joseph, Greenwich, will proved 1844. Children, Margaret and Joseph A.

Mary, Deerfield, will Nov. 13, 1811; proved Feb. 17, 1812. Children, Jacob, Joseph, Lawrence, Margaret, Mary, Catharine, and Simon.

Matthias, Deerfield, will Dec. 25, 1772; proved, Mar. 3, 1783. Wife, Marey. Children, Simon, Chrisson, Matthias, Cateron, Marey, Lawrence and Margaret.

Mathias R., Bridgeton, will May 8, 1859; proved June 29, 1859. Wife, Ann.

Nathan, Feb. 15, 1798; proved Oct. 1, 1798. Wife, Abigail Children, Joel, Abraham, Abigail, Nancy Platts and Sarah.

Samuel, Cohansie, will Oct. 12, 1780; proved Dec. 11 1781. Wife, Experience. Children, Noah, Joel, Israel and Lovice.

Susannah (widow of John), Cohansey, will May 18, 1749; proved June 3, 1749. Children, Elizabeth, Susanna and Jonathan.

William, Greenwich, will Oct. 12, 1802; proved Nov. 29, 1808. Children, William, Ebenezer and Elizabeth.

MILLS

Ephraim, Hopewell, will Sept. 8, 1776; proved Dec. 12, 1778. Wife, Rebeccah. Children, Ephraim, Uriah, Hannah, Maskell, Hope, Rachel Carl, Rebecca McLong and Philena Caruthers.

Richard, Hopewell, will Feb. 4, 1759; proved Aug. 15, 1767. Wife, Lydia. Children, Mary, Sarah Robbins, Paciance Sayre, Bethia Matthews and Lydia Yapp.

Richard, Hopewell, will Sept. 7, 1780; **proved Aug. 12, 1795.**

Wife, Elizabeth. Children, Elizabeth, Richard, Lydia Stockton, Abigail Ayars and Rachel McFerson.

Richard, Hopewell, will Feb. 27, 1797; proved June 12, 1806. Sisters, Elizabeth, Rachel and Abigail. Nephew, Azariah McPherson.

Samuel, Fairfield, will May 20, 1789; proved Mar. 29, 1790. Wife, Mary. Stepson, William Machesney.

MINCH

Adam, Hopewell, will Dec. 2, 1783; proved Jan. 2, 1784. Wife, Barbary. Children, Peter, Andrew and Benjamin.

MONTGOMERY

Robert, Fairfield, will Aug. 19, 1797; proved May 10, 1798. Wife, Pheabe. Children, William and Jean.

Robert, Fairfield, will Mar. 8, 1824; proved June 18, 1824. Wife, Hannah.

MOORE

Azariah, Stow Creek, will Aug. 6, 1804; proved Sept. 23, 1818. Sister, Bathsheba Hannah. Brother, Joseph Moore (dec'd). Sister-in-law, Ami, widow of Joseph.

Benjamin F., Fairfield, will July 4, 1854; proved Aug. 15, 1856. Wife, Amanda S.

Daniel, Deerfield, will Nov. 24, 1767; proved Feb. 24, 1768 Wife, Rachel. Children, Rachel, Daniel, Jonathan, David and Amey.

Daniel, Hopewell, will Jan. 8, 1817; proved May 22, 1817. Children, Phebe Cake, Sarah Fithian, Ann, Moses (dec'd), and John. Gandchildren, Almeda Moore, and William and George, sons of Moses Moore. Daughter-in-law, Eleanor, widow of Moses.

Enoch, Greenwich, will Jan. 27, 1775; proved Apr. 12, 1777. Wife, Rachel. Daughter, Rebecca. Sons mentioned, but not by name. Sister, Hannah Scott.

John, Hopewell, will Nov. 7, 1799; proved June 4, 1800. Children, Azariah, John, Lucy, Jacob, Eunice, and Hannah Shoemaker. Grandchildren, Elizabeth and Hannah Miller.

John Deerfield, will Oct. 1, 1846; proved Aug. 21, 1847. Children, Patience, Hannah Maul and John. Grandchildren, Jonathan, Elijah, Ann and John, children af son John; Jonathan, John and Phebe Husted, and Maria Garrison.

John, Bridgeton, will 1854; proved Oct. 4, 1854. Wife, Lydia.

Martha, Greenwich, will June 14, 1828; proved Oct. 13, 1830. Sister, Bathsheba Hannah. Neice, Martha, daughter of Bathsheba Hannah.

Moses, will Jan. 1, 1785; proved Dec. 4, 1795. Wife, Mary. Daughter, Sarah.

Phebe, Cedarville, July 25, 1848; proved Feb. 17, 1852. Brothers, Benjamin F. and Daniel Moore. Sister, Harriet Porter.

William, Downe, Mar. 12, 1787; proved Sept. 21, 1787. Children, William, Dicason, Edward, and Mary Ray.

William, Downe, will Mar. 13, 1817; proved Apr. 25, 1817. Children, Ann, Sarah Bacon, Dickinson, Edward, James, Mark, John, Daniel, and Thomas (dec'd). Grandchildren, Hamilton, Susannah and Thomas, children of Thomas.

MOSLANDER

William, will May 20, 1824; proved Feb. 27, 1826. Wife, Marjery. Children, Tabitha Bush, Abraham, Deborah Peterson, Elizabeth Christian, William, James, John, George, Thomas, Joseph and Daniel.

MULFORD

Aaron, Hopewell, will Nov. 29, 1750; proved Feb. 16, 1750/51. Wife, Christian. Children, Aaron, Moses, Daniel, Benjamin, William and Mary.

Benjamin, Bridgeton, will Aug. 16, 1784; proved Nov. 1, 1784. Wife, Hepsebeth. Grandchildren, Benjamin, Millisent, Margaret, Mulford and Samuel Dare.

Christian, Hopewell, will Oct. 7, 1752; proved Oct. 19, 1752. Children, Mary, Moses, Aaron, Benjamin, William and Daniel.

David, Stoe Creek, will June 4, 1829; proved Nov. 4, 1832. Children, Ephraim, Thomas, William, Rachel Cauch and Elizabeth.

George, Hopewell, will Jan. 14, 1781; proved Jan. 19, 1782. Wife, Christiana. Daughter, Elizabeth Rutter.

Henry, Greenwich, July 17, 1816; proved Oct. 10, 1822. Wife, Phebe. Children, Edward, Henry, Charles, Emma and Isaac S.

Isaac, Hopewell, June 27, 1776; proved Sept. 11, 1777. Wife, Sarah. Children, Isaac, Martha and Sarah. Daughter-in-law, Mary Coffin. Father, Stephen Mulford. Brother, Stephen Mulford. who has a daughter Sarah.

Lewis, Millville, will Sept. 28, 1841; proved Oct 23, 1841. Wife, Rebecca. Children, Rhoda, Mary, Tamson, Isaac B., Thomas, Furman and Lewis.

Margaret, Stoe Creek, Mar. 23, 1842; proved Apr. 6, 1842. Children, Phebe Maul, Precilla Minch (dec'd), John, Benjamin, and Mara, wife of Jonathan Bowen.

Mary, Stow Creek, will Jan. 23, 1822; proved Feb. 13, 1822. Children, Thomas, and Mary Barracliff. Grandchildren, Mary L. and Phebe, daughters of son Thomas Mulford, and David Randolph.

Moses, Greenwich, will July 8, 1760; proved Sept. 7, 1760. Wife, Rachel. Son, Joseph. Brother, Daniel Mulford.

Phebe (widow of Isaac), Stoe Creek, will July 10, 1855; proved Aug. 26, 1856. Grandson, Isaac M. Smalley.

Stephen, Hopewell, May 27, 1763; proved Aug. 20, 1763. Wife, Hannah. Children, Stephen, Isaac, Silas, Nathaniel, Ephraim, Henry, Sarah, Filathea and Rachel. Grandson, Thomas Mulford.

William, Greenwich, Feb. 28, 1801; proved Apr. 29, 1801. Wife, Sarah. Children, Timothy E., James W., Jacob, William and Maskell.

MURPHY

Prudence, Maurice River, will Dec. 15, 1846; proved Aug. 3, 1847. Children, William F., Naomi Tucker, Isaac, Hudson, Stephen and Jane.

Stephen, Port Elizabeth, will July 22, 1826; proved Dec. 6, 1826. Wife, Prudence. Sons, Richard and Stephen. Other children mentioned, but not by name.

MURRAY

Othniel, Fairfield, will Oct. 17, 1820 proved Dec. 2, 1820. Children, Sarah, Dorcas, Mary Ann, Mary, Mark, John and David.

NEWCOMB

Bayse, Fairfield, will Jan. 10, 1817; proved Jan. 23, 1817. Children, Ruth, Bayse, Nancy, William, Mariah, Daniel and Patience.

David, Fairfield, will May 30, 1812; proved June 19, 1812. Wife, Sarah. Children, Josiah, John Wesley, David and Clarenda.

Dayton, Fairfield, will Oct. 12, 1808; proved Apr. 28, 1809. Wife, Abigail. Daughter, Jane Harris.

Joseph, Downe, will Sept. 15, 1792; proved Aug. 16, 1793. Wife, Abigail. Children, Baze, Joseph, Elizabeth Brown, Sarah Westcott, David and Ethan.

Pleasant, will June 3, 1787; proved Apr. 8, 1791. Children, Butler, Nathan, David, Elizabeth, and Grace Page.

William R., Fairfield, will May 19, 1858; proved July 1, 1858. Wife, Jane. Sons, Benjamin and William.

NICHOLS

David, Deerfield, will Apr. 14, 1796; proved July 18, 1796. Wife, Mary. Children, Terne, Dan, Rachel Lawrence, Orpha Moore, Anne Garten, Josiah, Thomas, Meriam, Priscilla, Ishmael and Ruth.

Hosea, Cohansey, will Jan. 16, 1849; proved Feb. 5,,1846. Wife, Lurany.

Isaac, Deerfield, will Mar. 30, 1817; proved **Apr. 7**, 1817.   Children, Damaris Carll, Lydia Carll and Zachariah. Grandchildren, John and Mary Hannon.

James, Bridgeton, Mar. 23, 1842: proved Apr. 5, 1842. Wife, Jane.   Children, Adam, Isaac, James, Demaris Camm, Charlotte, Harriet, Eliza Garrison and Mary Frazure.

Jonathan, Deerfield, will Sept. 22, 1814; **proved** Jan 16, 1815. Wife, Rebecca. Children, Charles. John, Jonathan, Trivis, Mary VanMeter, Rebecca Mead, Rhoda Barton and Ananias.

Robert, Stow Creek, will Oct. 1, 1760; proved June 24, 1761. No relationship shown.

NICHOLSON

Esther, will Dec. 15, 1851; proved Feb. 25, 1852. Children, Philip Nicholson, Martha Goff, Caroline Goff, Jerusha Henderson, Thomas H. Nicholson (dec'd) and Esther H. Robinson. Grandchildren, Hugh H., Eleanor Riley, Martha Fuller, Lydia, Naomi, Thomas F. and Deborah W., childred of son Thomas; Charles W. and Edwin F. Lee and Ann Elizabeth Robinson, children of daughter Esther Robinson.

NIXON

Jeremiah, Fairfield, will June 2. 1798; proved Nov. 27, 1798. Wife, Hannah.   Children, Judith Harris and Theodosia Powell. Shn-in-law Pierson Harris.

Jeremiah, Jr., Fairfield, will June 22, 1812. Wife, Ruth. Children, Jeremiah, William, Reuben, George, Ruth, Naomi, Hannah and Elizabeth.

Reuben, Fairfield, will Oct. 22, 1773; proved Nov. 25, 1773. Brothers, William, Vavasur and Jeremiah. Sisters, Ruth Page and Susanna Nixon.

Seaborn Foy (widow of Jeremiah), will Oct. 23, 1773; proved Nov. 25, 1773. Children, Susanna, Ruth, **wife of David Page,** and William.   Grandchildren, Sarah and **Lovisa, daughters** of Lot Fithian.

Varvasur, will June 26, 1789; proved Sept. 26, 1789. Sister, Mary Nixon. Brothers, Oliver and Ephraim.

NORBURY

Joseph, formerly of St. Clements, in Liberty of Westminster, County Middlesex, England, son of Joseph Norbury of Little Shore Lane, in said parish, born in 1722. Wife, Lida. Children, Joseph, Heath and Mary. Will Nov. 15, 1769.

OGDEN

Benjamin, Fairfield, June 16, 1777; proved Apr. 24, 1778. Neice and Nephew, Rachel and Joel children of sister Rachel Westcoat. Brother, John Ogden.

Daniel, will Aug. 13, 1795; proved Sept. 22, 1797. Children, Charles, and Mary Garrison. Granddaughter, Priscilla Stedems.

David, Fairfield, will Nov. 19, 1759; proved, Dec. 18, 1760. Wife, Mary (lately wife of Thomas Bateman). Children, David, Nathaniel, Jason, Hannah, wife of Jonathan Lawrence, Hannah Jones, Elmer, Rachel Jameson, Abdon, Benjamin and John. Brother, John Ogden.

David, Fairfield, will Feb. 10 1765; proved Apr. 21, 1767. Wife, Sarah. Children, Norton, Mary and Sarah. Father, David Ogden. Father-in-law, Thomas Harris.

Hannah (widow of Jonathan), Deerfield, will Dec. 12, 1754; proved Jan. 6, 1755. Children, Richard, Jonathan and Joel.

Jason will Aug. 1, 1801; proved Aug. 10, 1801. Children, David, Mary Bishop and Jason.

Jason, Fairfield, will proved 1845. Wife mentioned, but not by name. Children, Burgin, Joanna, Susan, Nathaniel, Ephraim, Eber, Columbus, Jason, Mary and Elmer.

John, Fairfield, will May 6, 1759; proved June 21, 1759. Children, Zepheniah, Josiah, Samuel, Jedadiah, James, Elizabeth Shaw, Rhoda and Edward. Brother, David Ogden.

John, Fairfield, will Mar. 9, 1831; proved Aug. 22, 1832. Wife, Anna. Children, Abigail Westcott (dec'd), John, Rachel Lummis, David S., Hannah Howell, Abden, Elmer, Benjamin, and Matilda

Mattson. Gandchildren, Ephraim, Robert and Mary, children of Abigail Wesicott; Hetty, Lydia, John O., Nancy and Martha, children of Rachel Lummis; Emily and Matilda, daughters of Matilda Mattson. Brother, Elmer Ogden.

John, Port Norris, will Dec. 26, 1836; proved Apr. 23, 1838. Wife, Harriet. Son, Alfred. Other children mentioned, but not by name.

John B. will Oct. 4, 1813; proved Nov. 6, 1813. Wife, Sarah. Son, John. Sister, Sarah Ogden.

Jonathan, Fairfield, will Oct. 4, 1798; proved Dec. 7, 1798. Wife, Phebe. Children, Curtis, Edo, Betsey, Jane and Phebe.

Jonathan, Deerfield, will Feb. 20, 1812; proved Apr. 2, 1812. Wife, Martha. Children, David, Hannah, wife of William Reeves, Ruth, wife of John Garrison, and John. Grandchildren, David, Hannah and Esther Heward.

Joseph, Fairfield, will Sept. 15, 1737; proved Oct. 30, 1772. Wife, Abigail. Children, Joseph, Jonathan, Ruth Harris, Nathaniel and George.

Joseph, Fairfield, will Dec. 11, 1805; proved Feb. 11, 1806. Wife, Ruth. Children, Ruth B. Sarah, Nancy Pierson, John B., and an expected child.

Mary, Fairfield, will Mar. 14, 1763; proved Apr. 9, 1763. Children, Eleazar Smith, Martha Elmer, Rebecca Smith, Sarah Smith, Abigail Smith, Mary Banks and Esther Mayhew.

Nathaniel, Fairfield, will Apr. 6, 1767; proved Apr. 21, 1767. Children, Jeremiah and Phebe. Brother, Jason Ogden. Uncle, Joseph Ogden.

Sarah, Fairfield, will Jan. 14, 1793; proved June 10, 1805. Children, Benjamin S., Thomas, Ruth and James S.

Thomas, Fairfield, will Dec. 16, 1785; proved Dec. 30, 1785. Wife, Sarah. Children, Benjamin, Thomas and Ruth. Grandchildren, Thomas H. and John Ogden.

Thomas H., will Dec. 16, 1844; proved Sept. 17, 1847. Wife, Mary. Children, Thomas, Mary Westcott, Lydia, William, Harris and George.

William, Cedarville, will Apr. 20, 1850; proved July 9, 1852. Wife, Martha. Children mentioned, but not by name.

OSBORN

Ethan, Fairfield, will Oct. 6, 1850; proved May 11, 1858. Children, John, Anna Lawrence (dec'd), Ruth Thompson, and Robert. Son-in-law, Benjamin Thompson.

OTT

Martin, will Feb. 3, 1810; proved Nov. 2, 1811; Wife, Margaret. Children, Henry, George, and Catharine Sowder. Granddaughter, Catharine Sowder.

PADGETT

Elizabeth, Greenwich, will Apr. 14, 1838; proved Apr. 28, 1838. Neice, Priscilla, wife of Joseph Dare. Nephew, Robert Richardson.

Gabriel, Stoe Creek, will Apr. 12, 1834; proved Nov. 12, 1835. Wife, Luciana.

Mary, Stoe Creek, will Feb. 22, 1834; proved Jan. 5, 1847. Children, Daniel and David Mills.

Thomas, Greenwich, will May 31, 1832: proved May 10, 1835. Wife, Elizabeth. Brother, David. Sisters, Priscilla and Mary.

PAGE

Jonathan, will Mar. 22, 1777; proved June 24, 1777. Wife, Bethiah. Children, Jenathan, James, Hannah and Elizabeth. Brother, David Page.

Joseph, Fairfield, will Feb. 1, 1766; proved June 12, 1767. Children, Jonathan, David, Martha and Hannah. Grandchildren, David, Ambrose and John Page. Son's Widow, Mary Page.

PAGETT

Thomas, Stow Creek, will Jan. 20, 1748/9; proved Dec. 19, 1751. Wife, Dorothy. Children, John, David, Thomas, Mary Ewing and Abigail Harris.

PARIS

Peter, Deerfield, will June 26, 1812; proved Aug. 1, 1812. Wife, Susanna. Children, George, John, Gabriel, Daniel, Peter, William Joseph, Margaret, Susanna, Ann and Sarah.

PARKE

Thomas, Greenwich, will Mar. 13, 1764; proved Feb. 2, 1767. Wife, Sarah. Children, Sarah Isley, Martha Wolston, Prudence, Anna, Ananias, Rachel, Rebecca and Miriam

PARRIS

Christianna, Bridgeton, will Oct. 8, 1851; proved Nov. 24, 1851. Children, Catharine, Andrew, Susannah Callahan, Peter, and Phebe Westcott.

PARSONS

James, Downe, will Jan. 12, 1850; proved July 26, 1851. Wife, Margaret. Daughter, Susan Ann, wife of Sumner Tribbitt.

Jehu, Downe, will Mar. 10, 1830; proved Aug. 18, 1834. Children, Sarah, wife of Thomas Tribet, Jonathan, Nathan, James, Phebe, wife of James Bowen, John, and Lydia Hankins. Grandson, Elmer, son of Lydia Hankins.

Johannah, Downe, will June 12, 1836; proved June 28, 1836. No relationship shown.

Nathan, Downe, will Mar. 29. 1837; proved Sept. 4, 1837. Wife, Elizabeth. Children, Charles, James H., George, Isaac, Mary, Elizabeth and Dayton B.

PARVIN

Holmes, Deerfield, will Feb. 11, 1826; proved Nov. 8, 1828. Wife, Elizabeth.

James B., Fairfield, will Oct. 21, 1834. Children, Eliza M., James B., Caroline Howell and Charlotte Lummis.

James B., Fairfield, will July 15, 1851. Wife, Ann. Mother, Lovisa Parvin. Sisters, Charlotte, Caroline and Eliza.

Jeffrey, will Mar. 7, 1795; proved Apr. 11, 1795. Children, Salley, David, and Abigail Whitecar. Brother, Josiah Parein. Brother-in-law, Jedidiah Ogden

Jeremiah, Deerfield, will Feb. 3, 1780; proved Jan. 27, 1783. Children, Silas and Benaiah.

Jeremiah, Hopewell, will Dec. 6, 1816; proved Jan. 20, 1817. Wife, Sarah. Children, Sarah, Lydia, Harriet, Jeremiah and Anne.

Jonathan Fairfield, Sept. 14, 1841; proved Jan. 17, 1846. Wife, Amy. Children, Elam B., Nancy, Ruth Riley, Hannah McChesney, Daniel, Hiram and Horace. Grandson, Charles.

Josiah, Hopewell, will Feb. 6, 1758; proved Aug. 26, 1761. Wife, Susanna. Children, Lydia, Phebe and Josiah. Married daughters mentioned, but not by name.

Josiah, Bridgeton, will Aug. 12, 1822; proved Sept. 26, 1822. Wife, Mary. Wife's sister's daughter, Mariah, wife of Benjamin Whiteman.

Matthew, Fairfield, will Sept. 8, 1762; proved May 31, 1769. Wife, Sarah. Children, Thomas and Theophilus.

Theophilus, Fairfield, will Nov. 14, 1805; proved Dec. 12, 1805. Son, Theophilus.

PAUL

Hiram, Bridgeton, will Dec. 26, 1827; proved Apr. 12, 1828. Wife, Phebe. Son, Almarine.

PAULIN

Whitlock, Fairfield, will Dec. 14, 1759; proved Jan. 19, 1760. Wife, Rebecca. Children, Whitlock, Marget, John, Hannah, Elias and Jacob.

PAULLIN

William, Downe, will Nov. 10, 1773; proved Dec. 7, 1773. Children, Enos, Stephen, William, Alchy and Mary. Sons-in-law, Jonadab Sheppard and Stephen Cerbe.

PEARCE

Menan, will July 27, 1830; proved Jan. 27, 1832. Wife, Rececca. Sons, Morris and Richard. Daughter-in-law, Susy Gould.

PECK

John, Gohansey, will Oct. 18, 1745; proved May 1, 1748. Wife, Rebecca. Children, Jeremiah, John, Joseph, Abigail and Herbert. Granddaughter, Mary Ware.

John, Stow Creek, will Apr. 3, 1819; proved June 9, 1820. Children, Ann, Thomas W. and Martha.

Joseph, Deerfield, Sept. 3, 1776; proved Dec. 27, 1776. Wife Ruth. Brother, John Peck. Sister, Abigail Peck. Cousins, Jeremiah, Phebe, Rebecca and Hannah Peck. Stepson, Daniel Hannah.

PENNINGTON

Sarah, Greenwich, will June 22, 1805; proved, Aug. 19, 1805. Children, David and Isaac Bacon, Abigail McElroy and Rachel Rose. Grandchildren, Thomas R. Bacon and Elizabeth McElroy. Former husband, James Bacon.

PERRY

Amy, Bridgeton, will Apr. 13, 1832; proved May 3, 1832. No relationship shown.

Job, Fairfield, May 21, 1856; proved July 18, 1860. Wife, Rachel.

PETERSON

Aaron, Downe, will May 7, 1777; proved Sept. 13, 1777. Wife, Dorcas. Children, Amos, David, Ruben, Aaron and Rhoda.

Dorcas, will Sept. 16, 1805; proved Dec. 13, 1805. Brother, Nathaniel Diament. Sister, Rhoda Davis.

Isaac, Downe, will Nov. 24, 1813; proved June 30, 1821. Wife, Priscilla. Children, Priscilla, Ed, Ellis, Jacob, Isaac, William, Elizabeth French and Sarah Shaw.

Jacob, will Feb. 8, 1812; proved Feb. 17, 1814. Children, Peter, James, Elizabeth, wife of William Peterson, Jacob, Joseph and Abraham.

John, Maurice River, will Feb. 1, 1752; proved Feb. 24, 1752. Wife, Mary. Children, John, Dan and Ann. Daughters-in-law, Sarah Cobb and Abia Ganon.

PETTY

Elias, Fairfield, will Jan. 24, 1777; proved Nov. 28, 1777. Sister, Naomi, wife of Enos Seeley, who has children, David, Ebenezer and Ruth. Brother, Ebenezer Petty (dec'd), who has a daughter, Hannah Foster.

Israel, Jr., Fairfield, will Oct. 11, 1763; proved Oct. 28, 1763. No relationship shown.

Israel, Fairfield, will Feb. 9, 1765; proved July 3, 1767. Children, Elias, and Naomi Seeley. Grandchildren, David, Ebenezer and Ruth, children of daughter Naomi Seeley; and Hannah Petty. Son-in-law, Charles Howel.

PIERCE

Harvey, Bridgeton, June 15, 1850; proved June 28, 1850. Father, Richard Pierce. Brothers and sister, Hiram and Menan Pierce, and Angelina, wife of Uthniel Murry.

PIERSON

Azel, Stow Creek, will Feb. 3, 1765; proved Apr. 8, 1765. Wife, Mary Children, Ruth, Azel, George, Marce, Zeblun, Abigail and Rubin.

David, Fairfield, will Dec. 26, 1812; proved May 7, 1813. Wife, Hannah. Children, David, John and Eli.

Phebe, Bridgeton, Oct. 22, 1842; proved Dec. 2, 1844. Children, Daniel C. and Azel. Gandchildren, Azel and Phebe, children of Daniel; and Matilda Fithian, daughter of Azel.

PLATTS

David, Hopewell, will Oct. 30, 1801; proved Aug. 9, 1805. Wife, Latticia. Children, David Bacon, Jesse Platts, Jonathan, and Rachel Chroell.

Jonathan, Stow Creek, will Dec. 12, 1748; affirmed Feb. 18, 1748/9. Wife, Jean. Children, Thomas, Jonas, and Mary Evens.

Moses, Hopewell, will Mar. 20, 1775; proved Apr. 28, 1775. Wife, Patience. Children, David, Moses, Rachel, Mary (dec'd), Elizabeth, Phebe, Sarah, Judith, Rhoda and Daniel. Grandson, Jonah Terry.

Thomas, Greenwich, will May 21, 1759; proved June 21, 1759. Neices, Mary and Lidia, daughters of brother Jonas Platts. Cousin Jean, daughter of Jacob Evans,

POTTER

Sarah, Bridgeton, Sept. 25, 1820; proved Oct. 4, 1820. Children, James B., Robert, and Margaret Elmer.

POWEL

Richard, Fairfield, will Aug. 6, 1764; proved Oct. 3, 1764. Wife, Elizabeth. Children, Reuben, Richard, John, Elizabeth and Abigail.

POWELL

Daniel, Fairfield, will not dated; proved June 2, 1772. Wife, Abigail. Daughters, Violetta and Abigail. Wife's brother, Ephraim Harris.

David, Hopewell, will June 24, 1854; proved July 21, 1855. Wife, Rebecca Ann.

Ephraim L., Cedarville, will not dated; proved Oct. 5, 1858. Mother mentioned, but not by name. Brothers and sisters, Ethan O. Powell, Mary Thompson, Phebe Newcomb and Rhoda Fithian.

Henry, Fairfield, will Nov. 14, 1831; proved Dec. 2, 1831. Son, Henry.

Howell, Hopewell, Jan. 15, 1773; proved Jan. 23, 1773. Wife, Ann. Daughters, Ann Ware and Martha Powell. Grandsons, William and Howell Watson. Son-in-law, Isaac Watson.

John, Fairfield, Apr. 16, 1799; proved Sept. 26, 1799. Wife, Theodosia. Daughters, Violete, Abigil and Theodotia.

Reuben, Fairfield, will July 21, 1792; proved Mar. 28, 1793. Wife, Rhoda. Children, Rubin, Henry, Richard, Rhoda, Elizabeth and Abigail.

Reuben, Fairfield, will Oct. 22, 1830; proved Jan. 3, 1832. Wife, Mary. Sons, Ethan O. and Ephraim L.

Richard, Fairfield, will Feb. 24, 1781; proved July 7, 1781. Father, Richard Powell. Mother, Elizabeth Powell. Brothers, John and Reuben. Nephews, Reuben and Henry, sons of Reuben Powell.

PRENTZEL

Mary (widow), Deerfield, will Feb. 10, 1845; proved Apr. 15, 1845. Son, Charles Prentzel. Granddaughter, Mary P. Moore.

PRESTON

Ephraim, Fairfield, will May 20, 1823; proved Apr. 21, 1836. Wife, Sarah. Children, Jane White, Amy Houseman and Nancy Elmer. Grandsons, Ephraim D. and John E. White. Son-in-law, David White.

Hannah, will Jan. 12, 1782; proved Mar. 1, 1782. Children, Hannah, Elizabeth, Priscilla, Isaac, John B., David, Ruth and Barsheba. Brother, John Bower. Son-in-law, Ephraim Newcomb.

Isaac, Fairfield, will Dec. 16, 1748; proved Feb. 27, 1749. Wife, Elizabeth. Children, Levi, Isaac, William, John, Elizabeth and Joseph.

Isaac, Fairfield, will Jan. 8, 1775; proved Mar. 12, 1777. Wife, Hannah. Children, Bathsheba, Hannah, Isaac, John B., David, Elizabeth, Priscilla and Ruth.

John, Greenwich, will Jan. 18, 1856; proved Oct. 28, 1858. Wife, Hannah.

Levi will Feb. 19, 1750; proved Feb. 4, 1752. Daughters, Mary Bishop, Abigail Stratton and Freelove Dare. Elizabeth, widow of son Isaac. Grandchildren, Levi, William, John and Joseph, sons of Isaac; John, son of John Preston: Freelove, Thomasine and Elizabeth Stratton, Elizabeth Pierson and Mary Bennet. Sen-in-law, Samuel Bennet

PRICE

Aaron, Aug. 31, 1837; proved Sept. 26, 1837. Mother, Cintha Foster. Sisters, Grecian and Cintha Price. Brother, Jonathan Price.

William, Millville, Apr. 22, 1816; proved May 25, 1819. Children, Edward, Joseph, Mary Matthews and Deborah Stratton. Grandchildren, children of Mary Matthews by her first husband; Vartus, Mary, Rebecca and James Sweatman; daughter of Deborah Stratton, Sarah Stratton; daughter of Isaac Wynn, Rebecca Wynn.

PURPLE

John, Maurice River, will Aug. 8, 1749; proved Apr. 9, 1750. Children, Ponthenia Custalow, Marsey, and Abyah Peterson. Grandchildren, Catharin and Purple, children of daughter Abyah.

RAMSAY

William, Fairfield, will Oct. 24, 1771; proved Feb. 25, 1772. Wife, Sarah. Sons, James, Joseph, Ephraim and John. Brother, David Ramsay. Brother-in-law, Jonathan Elmer. Father-in-law, Ephraim Seeley.

RANDOLPH

Dorcas, Stoe Creek, will Aug. 11, 1811; proved Dec. 23, 1817. Children, Elizabeth Davis, Sarah, Beulah West and Richard F.

Martha B., Greenwich, July 10, 1848; proved Aug. 30, 1848. Daughter, Adaline J. Bacon.

Rachel F., Hopewell, will Apr. 5, 1800; proved May 24, 1806. Brothers, Elisha and Daniel Smith. Sisters, Abigail Biggs and Esther Davis. Nephews and neice Ami Castow; and Lazer, Noah, Nehemiah, William, Aaron and Ephraim, sons of Abigail Biggs.

RAY

Josiah, Bridgeton, will Aug. 17, 1843; proved Sept. 4, 1843. Children, Susan Wynn, Sarah Wynn, Henrietta and Maria.

READ

Charles, will Feb. 14, 1843; proved June 15, 1844. Wife, Margaret K. Sisters Margaret R. Eliza H., Dorothy and Martha.

Susannah, will Aug. 27, 1785; proved Dec. 20, 1785. Brother, John Clark.

Thomas, Hopewell, will Jan. 22, 1763. Wife, Susannah. Children, Thomas, Israel, Experience Miller, Patience Sayre; Rachel Miller and Mary Freeman. Sons-in-law, Annanias Sayre and John Miller.

Thomas, Hopewell, will Jan., 1779; proved Jan. 18, 1780. Wife, Rachel. Children, Israel, Mary, Ann and three daughters mentioned, but not by name. Granddaughter, Miriam Hinchman.

REED

Henry, Fairfield, will Sept. 9, 1766; proved Oct. 13, 1766. Wife, Phebe. Sister, Mary Page. Brothers, Daniel, James and Isaiah. Nephew, James, son of brother James Reed.

Isaiah, Down, will Apr. 26, 1796; proved Nov. 30, 1799. Wife, Amy. Children, Charles, Henry, and Naomi Newcomb. Grandson, Rusel Ladow.

William, Dividing Creek, will Nov. 25, 1760; proved Apr. 18, 1860. Wife, Dinah. Children, Dinah, Mary, Henry, Daniel, William, James, Isaias, Margaret and Prissillah.

REEVE

Joseph, will Dec. 31, 1760; proved June 7, 1763. Wife, Milysent. Children, Samuel, Joseph and Martha.

Stephen, will not dated; proved, May 29, 1855. Wife, Mary. Sons, Seeley P. and Thomas M.

REEVES

Abraham, Hopewell, May 18, 1761; proved June 9, 1761. Wife, Damaris. Children, John, Thomas, Abraham, Lydia Garrison, Sarah Moore, Abigail Miller, Hannah McGilliard and Stephen.

Damaris, Hopewell, will May 26, 1771; proved Dec. 13, 1771. Children, Abraham, John, Thomas, Stephen, Sarah Moore and Abigil Miller.

Elizabeth, Bridgeton, will not dated; proved July 31, 1834. Children, Abraham, Mary, wife of Uriah Gilman, Eunice and Rachel Reeves.

Henry, Maurice River, will Oct. 2, 1834; proved Dec. 22, 1840 Children, William, Abraham, Mary Marshall, Jane Ann Stanger, Dorothy Lafferty, Henry, Joseph and Elizabeth. Grandchildren, Jane Ann Marshall (late Stanger); Henry, son of Henry Reeves; Joseph, son of Joseph Reeves; Rebecca and Rachel, daughters of William Reeves; Jane and Eliza, daughters of Dorothy Lafferty; and William Smith Reeves.

John, will July 25, 1792; proved July 22, 1800. Wife, Mable. Children, Mable Leake, Eunice Bishop, Joseph and Abraham.

Joshua, Hopewell, will Nov. 16, 1836; proved May 9 1838. Wife, Rachel. Children, Thomas, Elizabeth Johnston, Catharine Forbes, Harriet Husted, Maria Harriet, and William G.

John, Hopewell, will May 24, 1806; proved Sept. 10, 1811. Wife, Martha. Children, Cornelius, Hannah, Ruth, David, John and Mary. Father, Thomas Reeves.

Juliana, Deerfield, will 1814; proved Mar. 10, 1818. Children, Prudence, French and James Reeves. Grandson, Edmund, son of James Reeves.

Mabel, Hopewell, will 1811; proved Dec. 1, 1813. Children, Mabel Leake, Unice Bishop, Joseph and Abraham.

Mark, Fairfield, Oct. 16, 1788; proved Sept. 11, 1790. Wife, Hannah. Children, Josiah, Mark and William.

Samuel, Stoe Creek, will Mar. 26, 1806; proved May 6, 1806. Wife, Mary. Sons, John and James.

Thomas, Hopewell, will Oct. 9, 1812; proved June 15, 1814; Children, Joshua, Thomas (dec'd), Sarah Parvin and Martha. Grandson, Thomas, son of Thomas. Daughter-in-law, Ruth, widow of Thomas.

REMINGTON

John, Hopewell, will Dec. 8, 1803; proved Nov. 6, 1810. Wife, Sarah. Son, John. Granddaughter, Eliza Remington. Son-in-law, Ephraim Terrill.

Moses, Greenwich, will Mar. 5, 1787; proved Apr. 9, 1787. Wife, Theodotia. Daughters, Rachel, Hannah and Sarah.

REMINTON

John, Hopewell, will, Nov. 3, 1766; proved Nov. 23, 1766. Grandchildren, John Reminton; Sarah Anderson; Moses, Thomas, Clement and Mary Reminton; William and Remington Ewing.

RENNELS

Silas, Hopewell, will July 4, 1806; proved July 26, 1806. Wife, Christena. Children mentioned, but not by name.

RIGANS

Lazarus, will Aug. 12, 1787; proved Sept. 25, 1787. Wife, Elenor. Five childred mentioned, but not by name,

RILEY

Elijah, Deerfield, will Dec. 8, 1852; proved Apr. 14, 1854. Children, Anna M. Parvin, Elijah D. and Enoch H. Riley.

Ephraim, Deerfield, will Dec. 5, 1840; proved June 14, 1843. Children, Mary Carnes and Ephraim. Grandchildren, Ephraim and Anne, children of Mary Carnes, and Sheppard, son of Ephraim Riley. Son-in-law David Carnes.

James, Jr., Bridgeton, will Jan. 15, 1827; proved Fob. 3, 1828. Brother, Joseph Riley.

Mark, Deerfield, will Nov. 8, 1785; proved May 2, 1795. Wife Prudence. Children, Daten, Ephraim, Elizabeth, Daniel, Ruth, James and Mark,

William, Hopewell, will Aug. 13, 1847; proved Sept. 1, 1851. Wife, Rebecca. Children, Jane, Elizabeth, Hannah Moore, Edgar Janvier, and a son eight days old, not yet named.

ROACAP

George, will Oct. 25, 1806; proved Dec. 6, 1806. Wife, Saloma. Children, Andrew, Adam, George, Catherine Shimp, Macklenah Johnson, Mary Weeks, Barbara Conover, Margaret, Jacob and Henry.

ROBBINS

John, Downe, will Oct. 4, 1777; proved Dec. 9, 1780. Children, John, Mary Robeson, Ruth Dollas and Rachel. Grandchildren, Robins and Web Robeson.

Levi, Downe, Mar. 11, 1859; proved Oct. 29, 1859. Wife, Silvey. Grandchildren, Levi, Sarah, wife of Peter Sharp, Daniel, Thomas, Mary, wife of Robert Robbins, Ruth, wife of John Blackman, and William H. Robbins.

Rachel, Stow Creek, will Jan. 24, 1795; proved Jan. 20, 1798. Children, Mary and John. Grandchildren, Rachel (dec'd) and Thomas Sheppard; and Thomas Mulford. Great-grandson, Daniel, son of Hannah Sheppard.

Richard, Dividing Creek, will Mar. 18, 1760; proved June 19, 1760. Wife, Sibbel. Daughters, Theodosia and Judith.

ROBBINSON

Rachel, will 1841; proved Sept. 12, 1849. Neices, Martha Demaris and Rhoda Woodruff.

ROBINS

Obadiah, Hopewell, will May 12, 1772; proved Mar. 11, 1775. Wife, Rachel. Daughter, Lydia Weathman. Sister, Hope Gardner. Son-in-law, Constant Weathman. Cousins, Richard, Samuel, and Obadiah Caruthers, James Gardner, Ellen Taylor, Hannah Bentley and Hope Fithian.

ROBINSON

Joseph, Hopewell, will Apr. 14. 1853; proved Jan. 31, 1855. Wife, Maleta.

Philip. Maurice River, will Nov. 29, 1855; proved Mar. 13, 1856. Wife, Judith. Children, Maurice B., Joel S., Ellen C. King and Sarah C. Lee.

Walter, Deerfield, will Nov. 23, 1820; proved Feb. 18, 1824. Daughter, Bathsheba Nichols. Grandson, Walter Nichols. Nephew, Bowen Moore. Neices, Phebe, Patience and Hannah Moore. Brother-in-law, John Moore.

William, will Jan. 11, 1777; proved Apr. 15, 1777. Children, William, Enos and Rhody.

William, Deerfield, will Mar. 17, 1788; proved Aug. 23, 17&. Wife, Sarah. Children, William, Ann, wife of Isaac Nieukirk, Mary, wife of Benjamin DuBois, Catherine and Rebeckah.

ROBISON

Reaves, Downe, will Sept. 9, 1843; proved Feb. 29, 1848. Wife, Christian. Children, William, Mary Coulter, Lovicy Smith, Harris (dec'd), and Christian.

ROCAP

Henry, Deerfield, will May 16, 1771; proved Apr. 7, 1772. Wife Barbary. Children, George, Henry, Catterein and Margaret.

ROCKHILL

Joseph, Hopewell, will Nov. 7, 1780; proved Mar. 27, 1788. Wife, Mary. Children, Robert, Samuel, Lydia, Clement and Mary.

RORAY

Benjamin, Cedarville, will Mar. 28, 1849; proved July 3, 1849. Wife, Hannah.

David, Fairfield, July 14, 1828; proved May 31, 1828. Wife, mentioned, but not by name. Children, Abigail, Daniel and David.

ROSE

Deborah, Newport, will June 12, 1849; proved Aug. 22, 1851. No relationship shown.

James, Fairfield, will June 14, 1749; proved Dec. 20, 1749. Wife, Elizabeth. Children, Phebe, Abigail Hays, James, Hannah and Elizabeth. Cousin Thomas Harris.

ROWELL

Thomas, Greenwich, will Apr. 10, 1773; proved Feb. 26, 1774. Wife, Elizabeth. Children, Cleffen, Thomas, and Hannah, wife of Solomon Poor.

ROYALL

David, Hopewell, will Aug. 4, 1807; proved Aug. 26, 1807. Wife, Ruth. Children, Joel, David, John, Susanna, Phebe and Polly.

RULON

Henry, Fairfield, will June 5, 1794; proved Mar. 7, 1810. Wife, Theodocia. Children, Moses, John, Jonathan, Ephraim, Benjamin, Henry, Abel, Anna, David and Nathaniel.

RUSSEL

William, Deerfield, will Mar. 28, 1772; proved Mar. 14, 1774. Sons, William, Daniel, Ephraim and Oliver. Daughters mentioned, but not by name. Grandson, Ebenezer Darvin.

RUSSELL

Ephraim, Deerfield, Apr. 10, 1791; proved May 17, 1791. Children, Robert, Joseph, Elizabeth, Achsah, Sarah, Adah, Lois, Ephraim and Thomas. Father, William Russell. Son-in-law, David Wood.

William, Fairfield, will Nov. 16, 1787; proved Mar. 9, 1789. Wife,

FROM CUMBERLAND COUNTY WILLS 109

Abigail. Children, Edward, Rebekah, Kezia, Mary, and Abigail Buck. Son-in-law Ephraim Buck.

RUST

Albert. Fairfield, will Apr. 7, 1767; proved Apr. 21, 1767. No relationship shown.

RUTTER

Jacob, Deerfield, will July 23, 1810; proved Aug. 22, 1810. Wife, Letitia. Children, Maria, Michael, Mary, Margaret, Elizabeth and Christenia.

RYLEY

James, Cohansey, will Apr. 7, 1755; proved May 19, 1755. Wife, Martha. Children, James, Jonathan, David, Nathan, Levi, Sarah Ogden, Elizabeth and Loramy.

SAUCOIL

Eve, Faireld, will Feb. 24, 1761; proved Aug. 18, 1761. Children, Jonadab, Leah, Rachel, Eve, Elizabeth, Lansalet, Experience and Patience.

SAYRE

Abraham, Deerfield, will Sept. 28, 1819; proved Oct. 26, 1819. Wife, Phebe. Children, Ruth, wife of John Newkirk, Josiah and Asa. Grandchildren, Caroline, Oliver and Lovina, children of Ruth Newkirk.

Ananias, Jr., will Jan. 15, 1772; proved Feb. 11, 1772. Children, Henry, Leonard, Phebe, Mary, Theodoshia, Rachel, Hannah, Lyddy and Rhoda.

Ananias, Stow Creek, will Nov. 26, 1785; proved May 24, 1786. Wife, Patience. Grandchildren, Theodosha Reminton, Mary and Charlotte Wood, Eli Elmer and Leonard Sayre.

Ichabod, Fairfield, May 9, 1772; proved June 23, 1772. Mother, Mehetable Sayre. Brother, Abraham Sayre. Sister, Athelah (?Alethea), wife of Daniel Garton, who has a son Gabriel.

Stephen, Hopewell, will Feb. 10, 1758; proved July 25, 1758.
Wife, Patience. Three sons mentioned, but not by name. Brother,
Ananias Sayre.

SAYRES

David, Fairfield, will Oct. 20, 1765; proved Apr. 25, 1767. Wife,
Lydia. Daughter Ruth. Brother, Thomas Sayres. Cousins,
James, son of James Sayres, and Anias, son of Daniel Sayers.

SCHENSER

Hannah, Bridgeton, will Sept. 26, 1821; proved Jan. 4, 1822.
Maria, Priscilla, Ananias G. and Jacob, children of Jacob Richer.
Neice Catharine Rose. Sister, Priscilla Moore.

SCUDDER

Samuel, will Mar. 8, 1796; proved Jan. 10, 1799. Wife, Sarah.
Children, Phebe, Salome, Elizabeth and William. Grandson,
William Smith.

SCULL

Silence, Greenwich, will Feb. 4, 1798; proved June 18, 1816.
Wife, Grace.

SEAYRS

Phebe, will Apr. 21, 1827; proved Sept. 28, 1827. Daughters,
Sally Johnston and Phebe Smith. Son-in-law, Aaron Stratton.

SEELEY

David, Deerfield, will May 8, 1802; proved June 16, 1802. Wife,
Nancy. Children, David, Hannah, Eden, James, Molly, William
and Edward.

Enos, Bridgeton, will July 21, 1843; proved Aug. 8, 1843. Wife,
Sarah. Sister, Naomi Ayars.

Enos P., Bridgeton, will June 7, 1846; proved Sept. 8, 1846.
Wife, Jane B. Children, Rebecca C. Ellet and Elias P.

FROM CUMBERLAND COUNTY WILLS

Ephraim, Hopewell, will June 18, 1774; proved Sept. 20, 1774. Wife, Hannah. Children, Sarah Ramsay, Esther Gibbon, Mary Elmer, Rachel Holmes, Hannah, Ephraim and Josiah. Grandsons, James Ramsay, Joseph Hall and Ephraim Ramsay. Sons-in-law, Jonathan Elmer, John Gibbon and Abijah Holmes.

Henry, Deerfield, will Sept. 30, 1767; proved Feb. 24, 1768. Children, Elizabeth Shute, Sarah Conklin, Hannah Bateman, Rode Nickles, Henry, John and Abigail. Grandson, Joel Moore.

Josiah, Bridgeton, will July 21, 1830; proved Mar. 20, 1832. Children, Richard, Mason G., and Robert. Grandchildren, James Josiah Ewing, William P., Charles and Henrietta Seeley.

Nancy, Bridgeton, will May 8, 1847; proved Apr. 14, 1849. Former husband, David Seeley. Son of former husband, William Seeley. Nephews, Leonard Woodruff, Andrew J., Ebenezer H. and Ephraim S. Swinney.

Richard, Stoe Creek, will July 16, 1845; proved Nov. 17, 1846. Daughters, Mary H. Tyler and Harriet Ware. Father, Josiah Seeley. Mother, Rebecca Seeley.

Sarah, Bridgeton, will Mar. 22, 1849; proved Apr. 5, 1849. Neices, Sarah, wife of William Wynn, and Susan, wife of Benjamin Wynn.

SHARP

Enoch, Downe, Feb. 29, 1848; proved June 14, 1848. Children, Peter, Parent, Hannah, wife of David Haley, Reuben, Enoch and Emily. Wife's father Reuben Lore. Father, John Sharp.

Lydia H., Downe, May 5, 1860; proved Oct. 5, 1860. Son, Coalman S. Sharp. Brothers and sisters, Joseph N. Richardson, Martha A. S. Rousman (nee Richardson), and Jeremiah Richardson.

Samuel, Mauricetown, will not dated; proved Jan. 23, 1860. Wife, Beulah. Children, mentioned, but not by name,

SHAVER

Adam, Deerfield, will Mar. 25, 1790; proved Oct. 12, 1790. Wife, Margaret. Wife's brother, Adam Tilsmires.

Jacob, Deerfield, will Apr. 10, 1774; proved June 25, 1774. Wife, Catharene. Children, George and Margaret.

SHAW

Abial, Fairfield, will June 28, 1781; proved Mar. 2, 1786. Wife, Abigail. Children, Pierson, Susanna Bower and Mary Lawrence. Sons-in-law, Jonathan Lawrence and Ebenezer Bower.

Carll, Fairfield, Mar. 26, 1750; proved Apr. 21, 1750. First wife, Hannah; second wife, Elizabeth. Children, Carll (first wife's son), Ryall, Hannah and Mary. Brother Joshua Shaw.

Henry, will May 7, 1781; proved Nov. 2, 1781. Wife, Elizabeth. Children, Leonard, Ira, Aaron, Henry, Susanna Daniels and Sarah.

Hosea, Fairfield, will May 2, 1807; proved, May 25, 1807. Wife, Rachel. Children, Ebenezer, Hosea, Abigail and Jerusha.

John, Hopewell, will Jan. 23, 1753; proved Mar. 2, 1753. Wife, Sarah. Children, Lucy, Temperance and Elishabe. Grandson, Jonathan Fithian, Jr.

Nathan, Maurice River, will not dated; proved Sept. 2, 1856. Wife, Elizabeth. Children, Benjamin F., Ruhamah, Nathan, Mary E. and Hannah M.

Richard, Maurice River, will Aug. 22 1758; proved Sept. 7, 1758. Wife mentioned, but not by name. Children, Richard, Jeremiah, John, Ichabod, Aaron and Nathan.

SHEPHERD

David, South Side of Cohansey, will June, 18, 1754; proved May 19, 1755. Wife, Sarah. Children, Ephraim, David, Joseph, Philip and Phebe.

David, Greenwich, will Feb. 10, 1770; proved Sept. 23, 1771. Wife, Ann. Children, David, Abell, Thomas, Lucy Bowen and Prudence. Grandsons, Dicason Sheppard and Benjamin Dare. Son-in-law, David Bowen,

David, Downe, will Mar. 20, 1773; proved July 21, 1774. Wife, Temperance. Children, Hosea, David, Oen, Jonadab, Tabitha, Temperance and Molly.

FROM CUMBERLAND COUNTY WILLS

David, Greenwich, will Apr, 29, 1777; proved May 13, 1778. Wife, Sarah. Mother, Ann Shepherd. Sisters, Prudence, wife of Jonathan Shepherd, and Phebe Dare, who has a son Benjamin. Nephew, Thomas, son of brother Thomas Shepherd; Brether-in-law, Nathan Shepherd. Father-in-law, Providence Ludlam.

Dicason, Fairfield, will Oct. 29, 1769; proved Dec. 6, 1769. Wife mentioned, but not by name. Children, Peter, Ansel, Dicason, Priscilla, Eloner, Sarah, Prudence, Pleasant and Hannah.

Dickason, Cohansey, will March 11, 1742; proved Nov. 28, 1749. Wife, Eve. Children, Patience, Stephen, Dickenson, Jonadab, Ann and Eve. Son-in-law, William Paulin.

Enoch, Hopewell, will June 29, 1769; proved July 27, 1769. Wife, Martha. Children, Lucy Smith, Furman, Dorcas, Elizabeth Robinson, Dorothy Brooks and Rachel Bacon.

Eve (widow of Dickason), will Feb. 4, 1849/50; proved Mar. 12, 1849/50. Children, Stephen, Dickason, John, Jonadab, Eve Sakel, Ann and Pesiains.

Jonadab, Fairfield, will Feb. 9, 1765; proved Apr. 9, 1765. Wife, Phebe. Children, Jonadab, Nathaniel, Read, Nathan, Silvanus, Temperance, Rhuma, Marah, Eve and Annah. Son-in-law, David Shepherd. Cousin, Able Shepherd.

Moses, Fairfield, will Nov. 15, 1752; proved Jan. 19, 1753. Children, Nathan, John, Moses, Rachel Reminton, who has a son Moses, Sarah and Mary.

Samuel, Fairfield, will Aug. 26, 1767; proved Mar. 22, 1768. Brother, Abraham; Cousin, Martha Brooks.

Silvanus, Cohansey, will Dec. 6, 1759; proved Feb. 5, 1760. Brothers, Samuel and Abraham Sheppard.

Stephen, Fairfield, will Oct. 20, 1757; proved Dec. 24, 1757. Wife, Ruth. Children, Joseph, Stephen, Peter, Gibbons, Martha and Lovice. Brothers, John and David Shepherd.

Thomas, Downe, will Feb. 2, 1776; proved Feb. 23, 1776. Wife, Ann. Children, Thomas, Isaac, Phineas, Patience, Eunice, Ann and Lucy.

SHEPPARD

Abigail, Greenwich, will May 14, 1804; proved Mar. 13, 1806. Children, Dickason, Phebe Davis, James, David and Abel. Grandchildren, Caleb, son of David Sheppard, Jane Ayars, Abigail, daughter of Abel Sheppard, Anna Davis, Abigail, daughter of David Sheppard, Rebecca, daughter of James Sheppard, and Abel Sheppard.

Abel, Greenwich, will July 1, 1772; proved May 4, 1773. Wife, Abigail. Children, Caleb, Dickinson, James, David, Phebe, Abigail, Ann and Rebecca. Brother David Shepherd.

Caleb, Greenwich, will July 24, 1834; proved Oct. 27, 1843. Wife, Edith, Sister, Phebe Davis. Nephews, Ivan and Abel, sons of Phebe Davis. Granddaughter, Hannah Ann Titsworth.

David, Downe, will Jan. 17, 1785; proved Nov. 28, 1785. Wife, Loruhama. Brothers, Jonadab, Owen and Hosea Sheppard. Brother-in-law, David Cheasmond. Uncle, Nathan Sheppard.

David. Jr., Greenwich, will Feb. 18, 1808; proved Mar. 6, 1812. Wife, Elizabeth. Children, Ephraim, Mary M. and Elizabeth B.

Edith, Stoe Creek, will Oct. 12, 1845; proved Sept. 17, 1846. Sisters, Claracy White (dec'd), Hannah Davis, Ann S. Swinney, Naomi Wood and Margaret F. Randolph. Nephew, David Davis. Brother-in-law, Reuben Davis.

Eleanor, Hopewell, will June 14, 1846; proved May 27, 1847. Children, Martha, widow of Lewis Randolph, and Caleb. Grandchildren, Thomas Tomlinson, Eleanor Sheppard, Lemuel Heritage and Edmund Davis.

Ephraim, Hopewell, will Apr. 28, 1783; proved Dec. 26, 1783. Wife, Rebecka. Children, Ephraim, Joel, Abner, James, Sarah Hannah Moore, Hope, and Rachel Sayre.

Hosea, will May 19, 1806; proved Jan. 23, 1807. Wife, Elizabeth. Daughters, Elizabeth Endicot, Prudence Robertson, and Temperance. Grandsons, Berzila Endicot, and Hosea, son of Prudence Robertson.

James, Fairfield, will Nov. 30, 1788; proved Jan. 6, 1789. Wife, Prudence. Brother, John Sheppard. Sisters, Mary Westcoat and Charlotte Sheppard. Brother, Jehiel Westcoat.

Job. Hopewell, will Mar. 22, 1796; proved Apr. 18, 1796. Wife, Rachel. Children, Job Lewis, Thomas, Rachel Dare, Mary Dare, Martha Thompson and Hannah Irelan.

Joel, Hopewell, will Dec. 1, 1819; proved 1820. Wife, Sarah. Children. Lydia Ayars, Dennis, Reuben, Amy Harris, Elizabeth Medcalf. Grandchildren, Naomi Youngs, Elijah Sheppard, Theophilus Davis. Sister, Sarah Hall.

John, Fairfield, will Oct. 11, 1774; proved Jan. 21, 1782. Children, Mark, Elias, Sarah Coles and Priscilla Moore,

John, Greenwich, will Sept. 27, 1794; proved Apr. 4, 1805. Wife, Priscilla. Children, John, Richard W. and Moses.

John, Greenwich, will Nov. 22, 1849; proved June 21, 1855. Children, Clarkson, Thomas R., Sarah, Mark M., Benjamin, Charles, and Priscilla W. Reeves.

Joseph, will Jan. 2, 1782; proved Mar. 21, 1782. Wife, Mary. Children, Isaac, David, Lydia, Ruth, Mary and Lucy.

Josiah, Fairfield, will May 25, 1795; proved June 25, 1795. Uncle, David Newcomb. Aunt, Grace Page.

Josiah, Hopewell, will Aug. 6, 1850; proved Aug. 16, 1850. Wife, Charlotte. Children, Henry, Hannah B. Glaspy and Harriet Kelsay. Grandson, Josiah Kelsay. Son-in-law, Ephraim S. Glaspy.

Jonathan, Fairfield, will July 29, 1758; proved Mar. 4, 1772. Wife, Elizabeth. Children, Jonathan, David, Ananias, Lawrence, Elizabeth and Rhoda. Cousin, John Shepherd, Jr.

Lawrence, Fairfield, will Sept. 30, 1822; proved Oct. 16, 1822. Children, Elizabeth, wife of Abner Woodruff, Rebecca, wife of Ezra Wood, Ruth, wife of Joseph Shints, Ellen, wife of Richard Downam, Polly wife of David Dunham, Lydia, wife of William Connor, Rhoda, wife of John Lore, and Nathan.

Martha, Hopewell, will Dec. 17, 1822; proved June 17, 1823. Children, Maria Harrow, Sarah Bacon, Nathan and Robert.

Moses, Greenwich, will Dec. 13, 1847; proved Feb. 10, 1848. Wife, Ann. Children, Rachel B., Mary Ann, Charles B., Edith J., and Ruth B. Cousin, Clarkson Sheppard.

Nathan, Hopewell, will Sept. 23, 1808; proved Nov. 2, 1811. Children, Nathan, Robert, Isaac, Martha and Molly.

Nathan, Fairfield, will Mar. 5, 1855; proved Mar. 20, 1855. Grandson, William H. Whitaker.

Philip, Deerfield, will Mar. 10, 1794; proved Jan. 31, 1797. Wife, Sarah. Children, Ichabod, Hervey, William, Mary, and Hannah Shaw. Grandchildren, Abigail Brooks, Prudence Johnson, Sarah and Martha Sheppard, and Joseph and Martha S. Newcomb.

Rachel, Greenwich, will Oct. 30, 1829; proved May 2, 1833 Sisters, Hannah Kelsay and Phebe Paulin.

Stephen, Back Neck, Sept. 22, 1783; proved Sept. 28, 1790. Brothers, Gibbons and Joseph Sheppard. Nephews and neice, Stephen Sheppard, and John and Hannah, children of Joseph Sheppard.

Temperance, Downe, will Feb. 19, 1814; proved Sept. 1, 1814. Daughter, Claricy Crandle. Father, Hope Sheppard. Mother, Elizabeth Sheppard.

Thomas, Hopewell, will May 5, 1798; proved May 24, 1798. Sister, Rachel, wife of Samuel Elwell. Neice, Hannah, daughter of Samuel and Rachel Elwell.

Thomas, Downe, will June 10, 1805; proved Jan. 8, 1806. Children, Abner, Isaac, David C. and Cintha.

SHIMP

Elizabeth, will Apr. 24, 1837; proved May 8, 1837. Children, Ann Miller and Jacob Reeves.

William, Hopewell, will Jan. 14, 1800; proved 1800. Wife, Mary Magdalena. Children, Lydia, William, John and Susanna.

SCHMIDT

Wilhelm, Stow Creek, Feb. 24, 1759; proved Mar. 6, 1759. No relationshrp shown.

SHOEMAKER

Henry, Deerfield, will Nov. 7, 1833; proved Nov. 27, 1833. Wife,

Rachel. Children, John (dec'd), Enoch G., Robert, George and Charles.

SHULL

Daniel, Newport, Aug. 25, 1852; proved Sept. 21, 1852. Wife, Rosanna.

Hoshel, Hopewell, will Dec. 26, 1825; proved Mar. 27, 1826. Wife, Margaret. Children, Samuel S., John P., Henry O., William W., Lydia Tice, Rachel Tice, Phebe R. and Henrietta Shull. Gandchildren, Edwin, Hannah and Rebecca K. Shull.

Jacob, Deerfield, will Aug. 20, 1785; proved Sept. 24, 1785. Wife, Rebeckah. Children, Azel, Jacob, Ruben, William, Susanna Parvin, Lovina Bateman, and Lydia.

Reuben, Deerfield, will Apr. 8, 1790; proved Sept. 29, 1790. Wife, Neoma. Children, Nancy and Jacob P.

Samuel, Deerfield, will Aug. 25, 1783; proved Sept. 12, 1783. Sister, Caterena Vanderford Cousins, Abraham Vanderford and Hosea Snethen.

SHUTE

Ann Elizabeth, Greenwich, will June 4, 1827; proved Aug. 28, 1827. Son, Charles Shute. Grandchildren, Ann Elizabeth Hanner, Ruth and Ann Elizabeth Shute.

Charles. Hopewell, will July 9, 1850; proved Aug. 7, 1850. Brother, Seeley Shute.

Samuel Moore, will Aug. 13, 1816; proved Sept. 2, 1816. Wife, Hannah. Brothers, Enoch and David Shute. Brother-in-law, Jeremiah DuBois.

SIBLEY

John, Bridgeton, will Apr. 24, 1826; proved Dec. 13, 1831. Wife, Sarah. Children, Rebecca, wife of James Westcott, John, Samuel S., Charles S, Sarah Smith, Jane B. and Martha H.

SILVER

Samuel, Port Elizabeth, will Oct. 21, 1828; proved June 2, 1829

Samuel, Port Elizabeth, will Oct. 21, 1828; proved June 2, 1829. Wife, Margaret. Sons, David and Isaiah.

SIMMONS

Thomas, Maurice River, will July 5, 1834; proved July 28, 1834. Wife, Ann. Children mentioned, but not by name.

SIMKIN

Dan, Stow Creek, will Feb. 15, 1775; proved Dec. 24, 1777. Wife, Marcy. Children, Hannah, Charles, Amos, and Letitia Sutton,

SIMPKINS

Dan, Bridgeton, will June 6, 1829; proved May 5, 1846. Wife, Rachel. Children, David P., Mary P. and Hannah M.

Francis, Stow Creek, will Sept. 5, 1755; proved Sept. 19, 1755. Wife mentioned, but not by name. Children, John, David, Abraham, Francis, Benjamin, Mercy, Rachel, Johanna, and an expected child.

John. will Mar. 25, 1786; proved July 10, 1786. Wife, Phebe. Children, John, Mark, Uriah, Silvanus, Hope and Hester.

SLEESMAN

Peter, Bridgeton, will Oct. 1, 1842; proved Feb. 21, 1830. Wife, Sarah. Sisters, Catharine, Hannah, Jane and Elizabeth.

Sarah, will Sept. 11, 1848; proved Dec. 18, 1848. Neice, Elizabeth, daughter of Philip Souder.

SMALLEY

Henry, will June 19, 1834; proved Feb. 20, 1839. Wife, Hannah. Children, William F., John and Henry L. Grandson, Holcomb Smalley. Wife's father, William Fox.

SMITH

Abner, Fairfield, will Dec. 12, 1855; proved Dec. 10, 1857. Children, George, Theodosa, James, Edmund, Aron, Theophilus.

FROM CUMBERLAND COUNTY WILLS

Abraham, Fairfield, will Oct. 25, 1770; proved Dec. 13, 1770. Wife mentioned, but not by name. Children, Nathaniel, Elias, Abraham, Sarah Mulford and David.

Alexander, will Dec. 17, 1751; proved May 19, 1758. Wife, Ruth. Children, Nathan, Alexander and John.

Eleazar, Fairfield, will Jan. 1, 1793; proved Feb. 17, 1797. Wife, Vashti. Children, Ephraim, Mary Westcott, Amey Stevens, and Alderman.

Elias, Cohansey, will Sept. 17, 1777; proved Dec. 20, 1777. Wife, Ruth. Daughter, Rhoda. Brothers, Nathaniel, who has a daughter Pheby; and Abraham, who has a daughter Elizabeth.

Elizabeth, Greenwich, will Mar. 12, 1852; proved Apr. 21, 1853. Children, David, Priscilla Pine and Mary M. Sheppard. Grandchildren, Hannah Ann Hannah, daughter of Ephraim Sheppard, Elizabeth daughter of son David, Rachel S. Pine, Edward M. Porter, Elizabeth Robinson, and Mary Jane and Emma Pine.

Elizabeth (widow of Ephraim), Downe, will Mar. 30, 1852; May 19, 1854. Neice, Charlotte Powell.

Ephraim, Newport, will Mar. 19, 1851; proved Dec. 27, 1851. Children Lummis, Mary Westcott and Ephraim. Son-in-law, William Westcott.

Isaac, Fairfield, will Feb. 15, 1794; proved June 2, 1794. Brother's widow, Bathsheba Smith. Brother's youngest daughter, Ann Smith.

Jabez, Deerfield, will Mar. 7, 1775; proved Sept. 8, 1777. Wife, Rebecka. Son, Daniel.

Jonathan, Bridgeton, will Aug. 20, 1838; proved Dec. 26, 1838. Wife, Sarah. Children, Phineas, Alderman, Asa, Jonathan G., Sarah Husted, Serenah Hann and Phebe Reeves.

Joseph, will July 1, 1807; proved July 18, 1807. Wife, Nancy. Daughter, Elizabeth. Wife's brother, Nathan Morrison.

Mary, Stow Creek, will July 9, 1774; proved Mar. 19, 1776. Children, Clark, Mary, Elenor Garrison, Charity Dunlap, Sarah Evans, Elizabeth Plummer and Hannah Dickson.

Nathaniel, Hopewell, will Aug. 19, 1772; proved Sept. 23, 1772 Wife, Naomy. Daughter, Phebe.

Richard, Stoe Creek, will Aug. 16, 1754; proved Sept. 16, 1754. Wife, Mary. Children, William, Ciark, Mary, Eleoner, Charity, Sarah, Elizabeth and Hannah.

Sarah, Bridgeton, will Aug. 18, 1801; proved Oct. 20, 1801. Children, John H. Ramsay, Ephraim Ramsay and Elizabeth. Grandchildren, Rebecca and Nancy Ramsay.

Thomas, Millville, will Apr. 3, 1816; proved May 11, 1816. Wife, Lydia. Son, James M.

William, Deerfield, will 1805; proved Apr. 5, 1806. Wife, Abigail. Children, Jonathan, Joel, Abner, Silas, William and Asa. Granddaughter, Sarah, daughter of Jonathan Smith.

William, Cedarville, will July 1, 1857; proved Oct. 2, 1860. Wife, Phebe. Son, William A.

SNEATHAN

Hosea, Deerfield, will May 11, 1829; proved May 14, 1830. Wife, Phebe. Father, Joseph Sneathan.

Phebe (widow of Hosea), Deerfield, will Feb. 21, 1840; proved Oct. 23, 1845. Brother, Nathaniel Foster. Neices, Hannah, daughter of Nathaniel Foster, and Elizabeth Garrison, daughter of Hannah McQueen.

SNETHEN

Ananias, will June 15, 1792; proved June 6, 1793. Wife, Rebecah. Sons, Joseph and John.

Joseph, will Jan. 11, 1786; proved Nov. 17, 1788. Children, John, Hosea, Annanias, Waitel, Zepporah Lawrence, Joseph and Phebe.

SNYDER

Anthony, Fairfield, will Aug. 27, 1856; proved Nov. 6, 1856. Children, David L., Sarah A. and Daniel B.

SOCKQUILL

Lancit, Fairfield, will May 3, 1759; proved June 8, 1759. Wife, Eve. Children, Jonadab, Lancit, Leah, Rachel, Eve, Elizabeth, Phebe, experience and Patience.

SOCKWELL

Lancet, Hopewell, will Aug. 2, 1736; proved May 3, 1793. Wife, Mary. Brother, John Sockwell.

SOMERS

Charles, Millville, will not dated; proved May 29, 1855. Wife, Sarah. Daughters, Lizia and Melicent.

SOUDER

Elizabeth, will May 23, 1827; proved Apr. 25, 1828. Daughters, Margaret Lummis and Mary M.

George, Deerfield, will Feb. 12, 1851; proved June 6, 1851. Wife, Rebecca. Children, Margaret Bowen (dec'd), Elizabeth, wife of Jonathan Garton, Catharine, wife of Hosea Garton (late wife of David Carll), Susannah, wife of Annanias Edwards, Martin, Ann, wife of James Harris, Mary Garton, Sarah, wife of Isarc VanMeter, and Rebecca.

John, Deerfield, will June 22, 1773; proved Aug. 9, 1773. Wife, Margaret. Children, Peter, George, Daniel, Jacob, Susannah and Philip.

Mary M., Bridgeton, will Feb. 9, 1847; proved Dec. 9, 1853. Sister, Margaret Lummis.

SOULLARD

Peter, Bridgetown, will Aug. 28, 1776; proved Jan. 12, 1784. Wife, Mary. Children, Peter, John, Jacob, Elizabeth Fox and Mary. Brother, Elias Soullard.

SOUTHER

Philip, Hopewell, will Mar. 16, 1769; proved Mar. 9, 1770. Wife,

Christena. Children, Peter, Philip, Simon, John, Mary and Susey. Son-in-law, George Miller.

SPENCER

John, Maurice River, will Mar. 20, 1846; proved Apr. 17, 1846. Wife, Lydia. Children, Jane Coombs (dec'd), Mary Lee, Hannah Horton, Sarah Padgett, Lydia Ann, Samuel F. and Eliza A. Getsinger. Grandchildren, Lydia Ann and John, children of daughter Jane.

STANFORD

Sarah, Millville, will Jan. 26, 1849; proved Aug. 21, 1860. Sisters, Christianna, and Mary Ann Avis. Nephews, Thomas and Francis Stow. Brother's widow Kesiah, wife of John Cobb.

STANGER

Jacob, Millville, Feb. 18, 1829; proved May 26, 1829. Children, Jane Ann, Susan, Francis, Mary Alfred and Ann.

STATHEM

Aaron, Greenwich, will Sept. 9, 1808; proved Nov 23, 1810. Wife, Susannah. Children, Grant, Esther Denny, Hannah Simpkins, Priscilla Jones, Elizabeth Dare and Sylvia Holland.

Deliverance, Greenwich, will Apr. 23, 1770; proved May 3, 1770. Children, Philip, Isaac, Aaron, Amos, Hannah Sayre and Sarah Bowen.

Grant, Greenwich, May 25, 1811; proved Aug. 6, 1813. Mother, Susannah Stathem. Nephew, William Richardson, son of Esther Esther Denny,

Hannah, will Jan. 28, 1789; proved June 15, 1789. Children, Thomas, Deliverance Ewing, Rebecka Dare, Dorcas Mills, Naomi, Philip and Ananias,

Isaac, Greenwich, will Feb. 1, 1776; proved May 3, 1785. Children, Jonathan, Mulford, Isaac, Aaron and Israel. Brother Aaron Stathem.

Jonathan, Greenwich, will Sept. 18, 1760; proved Mar. 7, 1763. Wife, Deliverence. Children, Philip, Aaron, Amos, Hannah Sayer and Sarah. Sister, Catharine Lester. Uncle Zebulon Stathem.

Thomas, will Apr. 12, 1749; proved Oct. 2, 1749. Wife, Mary. Children, Catherine and Jonathan.

STEELING

Jacob, Deerfield, will Oct. 7, 1805; proved Nov. 9, 1807. Wife, Sarah. Son, William.

STETHEM

John, Millville, will Oct. 24, 1857; proved May 14, 1860. Wife, Mary. Adopted daughter, Alice Stethem.

STEVENS

Henry, Deerfield, will July 13, 1753; proved May 25; 1755. Wife, Mary. Children, Jonathan, Ezekiel and Henry.

Samuel, Bridgeton, Mar. 1, 1803; proved May 14, 1822. Wife, Ruth. Wife's sons, Thomas and Richard Ross.

STEWART

John, Stow Creek, will May 27, 1796; proved May 15, 1798. Wife, Deborah. Son, James.

STILLE

Samuel, will Mar. 30, 1818; proved Aug. 11, 1818. Wife, Eleanor. Children, Nancy, wife of John McCormack, Lydia wife of John Ward, John, Hannah, Elizabeth and Jane.

STITES

Job, Greenwich, will Nov. 7, 1860; proved Nov. 28, 1860. Wife, Jemima. Brothers and sisters, Priscilla Osler, James, Levi, and Ann Heritage. Nephews and neices, Benjamin, Eliza, Kitturah and Mary, children of Priscilla Osler; Jacob Stites, Rebecca

Stout and Abigail Borden, children of James Stites; Job and Jacob, sons of Ann Heritage, and Levi, son of Levi Stites.

STOWMAN

George W., Maurice River, will Mar. 19, 1860; proved July 5, 1860. Mother, Eliza Stowman.

STRATTON

Benjamin, Cohansey, July 13, 1751; proved Sept. 18, 1751. Wife, Abigail. Children, Abigail Harris, Jonathan, Benjamin, Preston, Freelove, Thomasine, Elizabeth, Levi and John.

Daniel P., Bridgeton, will May 3, 1840; proved June 17, 1840. Wife, Maria. Son, John; other children mentioned, but not by name.

Elizabeth, Bridgetown, will Sept. 17, 1804; proved Sept. 25, 1805. Children, John and Powell Garrison Elizabeth Bowen, Ruth Nixon, Statia Garrison and Jemima Bacon. Granddaughter, Alvira Bowen.

Jeremiah, Millville, will not dated; proved June 6, 1851. Wife, Margaret. Children, William, Preston, Nathaniel, Thomas B. and Rebecca.

Thomas, Deerfield, will June 14, 1824; proved July 30, 1825. Wife, Margaret.

William, Deerfield, will July 30, 1759; proved Sept. 22, 1759. Wife, Phebe. Children, William, Jonathan, Sarah Parvin, Phebe Woodruff, Fithian and Aaron. Wife's daughter, Hannah Royal.

William, Millville, Apr. 30, 1853; proved June 15, 1853. Wife, Rachel. Children, William P. Frederick A., Joseph H., Caroline, wife of Isaac Brandriff and Hannah, wife of John J. Bates. Brother, Nathaniel Stratton.

STREEPER

Catharine, Bridgeton, will Apr. 17, 1835; proved June 25, 1835. Son, Clarence.

STRETCH

David, Fairfield, will Feb. 23, 1814; proved Mar. 4, 1814. Wife, Theodotia. Father, Bradway Stretch. Sister, Lydia, widow of Delaney Sharp.

STUDAM

William, Mauricetown, will June 24. 1857; proved July 14, 1857. Wife, Eliza. Children, Jane Ann, Charles, Sarah Elizabeth, Joseph and Emma Frances,

SUITER

Eliza, Greenwich, Mar. 15, 1860; proved Mar. 27, 1860. Neice, Anna M. Sheppard (formerly French). Aunt, Rachel Cox.

SUTTON

Joseph, Maurice River, will June 9, 1854; proved Aug. 25, 1854. Wife, Henrietta. Children, Eliza, widow of Reuben Tomlin, Susan, wife of John Wilson, Mary Ann Nottingham, Samuel, Rachel, wife of Ludlam Matthews, Joseph, Charles and Zabilla.

SWAIN

Joseph, Maurice River, will Aug. 30, 1811; proved Feb. 17, 1812. Daughter, Sarah wife of Dare Peterson. Granddaughter, Hannah, daughter of Dare and Sarah Peterson.

Richard, Maurice River, will Dec. 22, 1807; proved June 3, 1808. Brother Nathan Swain. Wife and sister, deceased.

SWING

Michael, Fairfield, will Dec. 13, 1833; proved Feb. 13, 1834. Wife, Susanna. Son, Charles. Other children mentioned, but not by name.

SWINNEY

Deborah, Hopewell, will Apr. 27, 1758; proved May 8, 1760. Children, Joseph, Deborah Bower and Ann Ayres. Grandchildren, Sarah, Jess, Joseph, Elisha, Ruth, Valentine and Mary.

Elisha, Hopewell, will June 7, 1796; proved Aug. 10, 1796. Wife, Eunice. Children, David, John, Daniel, Rachel, Ruth and Martha.

John, Hopewell, will Feb. 9, 1756; proved Apr. 16, 1756. Wife, Martha. Children, Elisha, Valentine, Rachel, Ruth and Mary.

TAYLOR

George, Downe, will Feb. 6, 1841; proved Feb. 21, 1843. Wife, Lydia. Son, Matthias. Grandchildren, Lydia daughter of Matthias, and Thomas Jefferson, son of James Lore.

William, Fairfield, will Jan. 23, 1843; proved Feb. 8, 1843. Wife, Nancy. Daughter, Harriet, wife of Harrison Westcott.

TERRY

Richard, will Dec. 19, 1770; proved Dec. 24, 1770. Wife, Elizabeth. Children, Ephraim, Nathan, Rebekah, Daniel, Jeremiah, Ashbery, Laurea, Sarah and Letcher.

TEST

Ann, Greenwich, will Feb. 27, 1843; proved May 3, 1851. Children, John, Joseph D., Richard W., Francis (dec'd), Ann F., wife of James Lane, Margaret and Latitia. Grandchildren, Sarah A., John and Elizabeth L., children of Francis Test.

Benjamin, Deerfield, will Feb. 1, 1801; proved July 12, 1802. Wife, Elizabeth. Children, David, Sarah Huggins, Zaccheus, Deborah Thompson and Elizabeth Gruff.

THOMAS

Ezekiel, Bridgeton, June 12, 1830; proved Sept. 21, 1830. Children, James, Levi, Samuel, Ezekiel, Phoebe Ayres, Sarah Harris and Tirza Harris.

Rachel, Bridgeton, will Mar. 16, 1831; proved Apr. 30, 1831. Son, David, and Sarah, his wife.

THOMPSON

Benjamin, Sr., will Sept. 27, 1785; proved Feb. 1, 1786. Wife,

Hester   Children, Benjamin, Elijah, Patience, Elizabeth and Priscilla.

Butler, Fairfield, will Feb. 5, 1791; proved July 23, 1791.   Children, Mary and Ann.

John, will May 24, 1816; proved June 19, 1816.   Wife, Martha. Children, Francis, Elizabeth, William, Anne, John and Thomas.

Warren, will not dated; proved Jan. 5, 1854.   Wife, Elizabeth. Children, Warren, Barlow, Mehitable Kane, Hugh and Anson. Grandchildren, Sarah Edwards, Elizabeth Hankins and Benajah Thompson.

TILLEGROVE

Benjamin, Springtown, will July 6, 1852; proved Oct. 22, 1852. Wife, Eliza. Children, Margaret, wife of Perry Johnson, Frederick, John and Immanuel.

TILSILVER—Tilshofer

Michael, Stow Creek, will Aug. 16, 1753; proved Sept. 19, 1753. Wife, Elizabeth. Children, Martin, Simon, John, George, Margaret, Christian and Jacob.

TOMLINSON

James, Hopewell, will June 29, 1810; proved June 5, 1811. Wife, Dorothy. Children. Nathan, Samuel, Thomas, and Margaret Davis. Son-in-law, Ebenezer Davis.

TOZER

Jeremiah, Maurice River, will Nov. 20, 1839; proved, Nov. 13 1845. No relationship shown.

TRENCHARD

Curtis, Fairfield, will Sept. 25, 1837; proved Apr. 23, 1840. Children, George O., and Mary B. Ogden. Grandchildren, Curtis James Trenchard, Thomas Harris Ogden and Theodosia T. Ogden.

TUBMAN

Silvanus, Downe, will Sept. 12, 1816; proved Jan. 17, 1817. Wife, Theodoshea. Children, John, Neamiah, Ruth Ladow and Soviah Orr.

TYLER

Benjamin, Greenwich will Oct. 29, 1773; proved Apr. 16, 1774. Wife, Mary. Children, John, Job, Burgin, Elizabeth Dunnum, Rachel Reeve, Latitia, Liddia and Hannah.

Samuel, Greenwich, will July 23, 1846; proved May 7, 1849. Children, Benjamin (dec'd), Samuel, Rachel, wife of Aulay Wood, and George B.

VANDERFORD

Abigail, Fairfield, will Mar. 14, 1842; proved Aug. 20, 1844. Children, John P. Newcomb, James R. Newcomb, and Elizabeth P. Blizzard.

John, Fairfield, will Aug. 18, 1824; proved Jan. 30, 1840. Wife, Abigail. Son, Abraham.

VANDYKE

Nicholas, Fairfield, will Jan. 15, 1777; proved June 19, 1777. Wife, Sarah. Daughters, Rachel Stevenson and Mary Crossley.

VANEMAN

Christianna, Port Elizabeth, will Dec. 5, 1845; proved Dec. 23, 1845. Children, Jacob, Polly Dare and Betsey Murphy. Granddaughters, Margaret, daughter of Jacob Vaneman, and Christianna Vaneman.

VANHOOK

Benjamin R., will Sept. 13, 1839; proved Nov. 29, 1839. Son, William B.

VANNAMAN

David, Maurice River, will Aug. 20, 1792; proved Mar. 30, 1793

Children, Richard, Lydda Freeland, Juda Lock and Margit Lock. Grandson, David, son of Richard Vanaman.

VICKERS

Philipp, Cohansey, will Feb. 17, 1758; proved Mar. 22, 1758. Wife, Sarah. Daughter, Mary. Son-in-law, Edmond Dare. Daughter-in-law, Ann Dare.

WAGONER

William, Bridgeton, will Jan. 26, 1772; proved Feb. 6, 1772. Wife, Margaret. Children, Margaret and George. Nephew, William Sailer. Brothers-in-law, Zachariah Sailer.

WAITHMAN

Thomas, Stow Creek, will Apr. 6, 1808; proved Dec. 21, 1809. Wife, Mary. Children, Ruth Loper and John.

William, Greenwich, will May 4, 1776; proved May 20, 1776. Wife, Sarah. Daughters, Sarah and Hannah. Wife's son, David Bacon.

WALLING

Jonathan, Greenwich, will Feb. 8, 1769; proved Mar. 18, 1769. Wife, Mary. Children, Ladus, Jonathan, Cynthus and Mary.

Ladis, Greenwich, Nov. 18, 1787; proved Dec. 1, 1787. Children, Jonathan, Ladis and Joseph. Mother-in-law, Rebecca Brewster.

Mary, Greenwich, will July 9, 1771; proved Aug. 16, 1771. Children, Ladis, Jonathan, Mary and Cynthus. Nephew, John Watson. Brother, Isaac Watson.

Thomas, Cohansey, will Oct. 6, 1747; proved June 7, 1748. Wife, Sarah. Children, Anna, Mary, Jonathan and Thomas.

Thomas, will not dated; proved Oct. 10, 1761. Wife, Sarah. Brother, Jonathan Walling. Sister, Mary.

WARD

Samuel, Greenwich, will Jan. 1, 1774; proved Mar. 7, 1774. Wife, Phebe. Nephew, Stephen Ranny.

WARE

Job, Greenwich, will Mar. 14, 1806; proved Apr. 1807. Wife, Hope. Children, Mary, Rachel Bacon and Isaac F. Brother, Mark Ware. Brother-in-law, Isaac Fithian.

John, Greenwich, will Apr. 11, 1773; proved Apr. 29, 1773. Wife, Anna. Children, Rachel, Anna, John, Job, Lattin and Mark.

John, Bacons Neck, will Oct. 7, 1806; proved Feb. 12, 1807. Wife, Elizabeth. Children, Elizabeth, Margaret, Caleb, John and Newton.

Josiah, Cohansey, will Apr. 23, 1749; proved May 19, 1749. Brother, Thomas. Sisters, Phebe, Amey and Elizabeth.

Maskell, will June 15, 1845; proved Feb. 26, 1846. Wife, Hannah. Children, Ruth Applegate, Maskell, William, Thomas and John.

Thomas, Stow Creek, will May 24, 1769; proved July 1, 1769. Children, Jacob, Thomas, Isaac, Enoch, Priscilla, Amme, Hannah and Lydia. Father, Jacob Ware.

Thomas, Stoe Creek, will Dec. 9, 1854; proved Jan. 17, 1855. Son, Ebenezer.

William, will Mar. 5, 1852; proved May 31, 1852. Wife, Jane. Daughter, Harriet B., wife of Jesse D. Claypoole.

WATSON

Isaac, Greenwich, will July 27, 1810; proved Mar. 11, 1811. Children, Howell P. and Sarah. Neice, Sarah Maskell. Nephew, Samuel, son of Samuel Watson, and Thomas Watson, who has daughters, Rebecca, Hannah and Jane. Brother Samuel Watson.

Samuel, Greenwich, will Aug. 18, 1778; proved Dec. 16, 1778. Children, Thomas, Samuel, Lemuel, Ruth and Rachel. Brother, Isaac Watson.

Sarah, Greenwich, will Apr. 5, 1842; proved Apr. 20, 1846. Children, William and Lydia L. Father, Providence Ludlam (dec'd). Grandchildren, Sarah W. and Elizabeth Miller; Sarah L., Charles and Howell P. Watson; Richard L. W., Priscilla S. and Lydia W. Probasco.

WEBB

Alexander, Bridgeton, will May 7, 1849; proved July 30, 1849. Wife, Maria. Father-in-law, Daniel Pierson.

WELDON

Joseph, Maurice River, will Oct. 7, 1857; proved June 9, 1860. Wife, Mary. Son, James. Other children mentioned, but not by name,

WELSH

John, Greenwich, will not dated; proved May 2, 1847. Wife, Eliza Ann. Daughters, Ann W. and Lydia S.

WESCOTE

David, Fairfield, will May 29, 1772; proved Aug. 12, 1772. Wife, Susannah. Children, David, Abinadab, John, Rhoda and Rachel.

Ebenezer, Cohansey, will Feb. 1, 1772; proved Mar. 16, 1772. Wife, Phebe. Sons, Ebenezer and Philip.

Henry, Fairfield, will Feb. 14, 1760; proved Mar. 8, 1760. Wife, Sarah. Children, Amos, Lewis, Ezra and Josh.

Joseph, Fairfield, will June 6, 1777; proved June 24, 1777. Wife, Mary Children, Joseph, Levi, Ephraim, and an expected child.

WEST

Jacob, Stoe Creek, will March 13, 1834; proved Nov. 28, 1834. Wife, Eunice. Sons, Samuel and Joseph. Grandson, Isaac West.

WESTCOT

Ebenezer, Fairfield, will Jan. 7, 1748/9; proved Feb. 24, 1748/9. Wife, Barbary. Children, Ebenezer, Foster, Samuel, Jonathan, David, Joseph, Abigail, Rode. Mary, Phebe and Joanna.

WESTCOTT

David, Fairfield, will July 26, 1803; proved Nov. 28, 1804. Wife,

Mary. Children, David, Nancy, Judith and Phebe. Brother, Sheppard Westcott.

Ezekiel, Fairfield, will Aug. 17, 1829; proved Dec. 15, 1831. Children, Nancy Ward, Ruth Husted, William, Ezekiel, Jehu and Rebecca. Grandson Stephen G. Clark.

Jonathan, Sayres Neck, will June 16, 1840; proved Jan. 5, 1852. Daughters, Abigail, and Jane, wife of John P. Moore.

Nancy, Bridgeton, will Mar. 23, 1836; proved May 20, 1837. Children, Isaac H. Hampton, Ruth Jeffers, Maria Brewster and Margaret Howell. Granddaughter, Ann Brewster.

Philip, Fairfield, will Apr. 11, 1806; proved Apr. 30, 1806. Wife, Esther. Children, Ebenezer, William, Philip, Elizabeth and Phebe. Brother, Sheppard Westcott. Wife's son, Benjamin Elmer.

Sheppard B., Bridgeton, will May 13, 1853; proved July 20, 1853. Wife, Phebe. Children, Francis W. and John P.

William, Cedarville, will Feb. 6, 1852; proved Feb. 20, 1852. Children, Caroline and William. Son-in-law, Franklin Lawrence.

WHEATON

Anna, Hopewell, will Feb. 20, 1829; proved Mar. 12, 1829. Children, Isaac, Reuben, Ann, Rhoda, Caroline, Mary and Ruth. Brother, John Laning.

Isaac, Hopewell, will June 12, 1761; proved Mar. 22, 1762. Wife, Hannah. Children, Isaac, John, Bagley, Reuben, Charles, Hepzibah, Sarah and Hannah. Brother-in-law, Enos Woodruff.

John, Stow Creek, will Mar. 1, 1780; proved July 2, 1783. No relationship shown.

John, Hopewell, will Sept. 23, 1856; proved Oct. 20, 1856. Daughter, Phebe Ann, wife of Zebedee Clement.

Jonathan, Greenwich, will Nov. 21, 1794; proved Dec. 18, 1794. Children, Eli and Priscilla.

Judith, Hopewell, will Jan. 12, 1822; proved May 9, 1822. Children, Judith Tomlinson, William and Jacob. Father, Providence

Ludlam. Gandchildren, Isaac W. and Adeline Harris; Mary and Isaac, children of Jacob Wheaton.

Noah, Hopewell, Dec. 13, 1760; proved Jan. 31, 1761. Wife, Elizabeth. Children, Robert, Henry, Sarah Reed, Mary, Martha and Jonathan.

Noah, Sr., Hopewell, will Feb. 13, 1772; proved Apr 4, 1772. Children, Daniel, Nansey, Massey, Noah and Elijah.

Robert, Hopewell, will Mar. 27, 1818; proved Sept. 21, 1818. No relationship shown.

WHETEN

Joseph, Greenwich, will Feb. 19, 1753; proved Feb. 12, 1767. Wife, Mary. Daughter, Priscilla. Sisters, Elizabeth Dun and Rachel Hudson.

WHITACAR

Lewis, Fairfield, will not dated; proved Oct. 22, 1773. Wife, Anna. Daughter, Lydia. Other children mentioned, but not by name. Brother, Ambrose Whitacar.

WHITAKER

Isaac, Bridgeton, will Oct. 29, 1856; proved Mar. 5, 1857. Children, Oliver, Enoch, James, Isaac, Ann, wife of Henry Burton, Sarah Smith, Caroline VanMeter, Lydia and Louis. Son-in-law, Edward VanMeter.

Nathaniel, Fairfield, will Dec. 13, 1752; proved Jan. 19, 1753. Children, Ambrose, Lemuel, Lewis, Daniel, Sarah, Hannah and Ruth.

Richard, Fairfield, will June 25, 1759; proved July 18, 1759. Wife, Elizabeth. Children, Richard, Lawrana, Elizabeth, Vashti, Susanna, Lydia, Elnathan and Reuben.

WHITE

Jennings, Deerfield, will Apr. 28, 1808; proved Sept. 27, 1808. Wife, Prudence. Children, James, Susannah, Phebe, Elizabeth, Rebecca, Hannah and Prudence. Grandson, James Shoemaker.

WHITECAR

Joseph, Downe, will Apr. 22, 1777; proved Sept. 18, 1779. Wife, Abigail. Children, Benjamin, Samuel, Abigail Barreen, Ruth, Amay and Elias. Grandson, Joseph.

Thomas, Fairfield, will May 25, 1779; proved Nov. 30, 1779. Wife, Bathnifle. Children, David, Jeremiah, Thomas, Diament, Priscilla Ann Youstead and Mary Pearson. Granddaughter, Rhoda Powell.

WHITEKAR

Carll, Fairfield, will Sept. 26, 1816; proved Oct. 25, 1824. Nephews, Carll and Thomas, sons of John Whitekar; and Franklin, son of Silas Whitekar. Neices, Dorcas, wife of Samuel Jenkins, Rebecca, wife of Claudius Long, and Mary and Sarah daughters of John Whitekar.

Elas, Downe, will May 3, 1777; proved Nov. 17, 1778. Wife, Margrat. Son, Joseph.

John, Fairfield, will Sept. 25, 1773; proved Oct. 23, 1773. Wife mentioned, but not by name. Children, Thomas, John, James, Silas and Carll.

Lydia, Fairfield, will Oct. 31, 1822; proved Nov. 8, 1830. Children, Anna Bishop, Lydia Craig, Joel, Ruel and Nathaniel. Niece, Harriet Bond.

Silas, Fairfield, will Mar. 28, 1804; proved Sept. 27, 1804. Son, Franklin. Brother, Carll Whitekar.

WHITICAR

Elnathan, will Aug. 14, 1794; proved Oct. 13 1795. Wife, Tamson. Daughter, Elizabeth. Brother, Richard Whiticar.

Michael, Fairfield, will Sept. 11, 1856; proved Feb. 3, 1857. Wife, Ellen. Father, Ephraim Whiticar. Brothers, George S. and Allen Whiticar. Sisters, Elizabeth and Emily Whiticar.

WICKWARD

Samuel, will Aug. 25, 1807; proved Feb. 16, 1808. Wife, Sarah.

Children, Allin, John, Deborah, Sarrah, Charrite, Rebeckah and Mary.

WILLIAMS

James, will Oct. 7, 1828; proved Apr. 27, 1830, Wife, Rebecca. Grandson, James W. Harris.

Thomas, Fairfield, will Dec. 25, 1794; proved Feb. 18, 1796. Wife, Mary. Daughters, Ruth and Margrit.

Whitefield, Maurice River, will June 8, 1816; proved July 5, 1816. Wife, Rhoda. Grandmother, Thankful Williams.

WILSON

Joseph, Greenwich, will not dated; proved Oct. 20, 1853. Wife, Sarah. Son, Richard.

Elias, will Feb. 9, 1828; proved Feb. 25, 1828. Wife, Ruth. Children, Jane Ann, Abigail Mary, Mary Foster, Elias, and Marthew Duffee.

WOOD

Aulay M. C., Stow Creek, will May 13, 1845; proved May 13, 1853. Sons, David and Aulay B.

David, Stow Creek, will Mar. 10, 1794; proved Jan. 18, 1798. Wife, Elizabeth. Children, Obadiah, Sarah, Prudence, Lucy, John, James, Phebe, Lydia, David and Aulay McC.

Elizabeth, Hopewell, will Sept. 23, 1839; proved Oct. 14, 1839. Grandchildren, Elizabeth and Mary Frances Paulin.

Hannah, Deerfield, will May 15, 1826; proved Jan. 23, 1827. Children, Hannah Evans and John Grandchildren, Hannah D. and Elizabeth W. Lummis.

James, Bridgeton, will Apr. 11, 1834; proved Apr. 30, 1834 Wife, Laranah. Son, James.

Joel, will Dec. 17, 1814; proved Feb. 24, 1815. Wife, Elizabeth. Children, Sarah, William, Eli and Job S.

John, Stoe Creek, will July 2, 1817; proved Oct. 13, 1819. Wife, Lucy. Son, John S. Grandsons, John W. and Thomas A. Maskell.

Jonathan, Deerfield, will July 11, 1802; proved Sept. 22, 1802 Wife, Reumah. Children, Biney, Ann Jones, Hannah Duffel and Mary.

Mary, Greenwich, will Jan. 14, 1814; proved Jan. 7, 1817. Children, Elizabeth, Job Bacon and George Bacon. Grandchildren, Elizabeth Hall, Sarah Sheppard, Charles Stewart and Eliza Ann Bacon.

Nathan Deerfield, will Apr. 14, 1751; proved June 14, 1751. Brothers, Elnathan and Job Wood. Sister, Mary Brual.

Rachel, Stow Creek, will July 9, 1793; proved Aug. 10, 1796. Sisters, Sarah Houseman and Hannah Bennett. Brother-in-law, Leonard Bennett.

Richard, Greenwich, will Jan. 4, 1802; proved June 19, 1807. Wife, Mary. Sons, Richard and James.

Richard, Greenwich, will July 10, 1819; proved Jan. 23, 1822. Children, David C., George B., Richard D., Charles S., Horatio C., Ann Elizabeth and Hannah D.

Richard, Millville, will Aug. 30, 1831; proved Sept. 10, 1831. Wife, Mary. Mother, Priscilla Wood.

Walter, Stow Creek, will Feb. 20, 1814; proved May 21, 1814. Wife, Anna. Sons, Ezra, Joel, Eli and Sheppard. Grandchildren, Sarah Wood and Jobe.

WOODNUTT

Comfort, will Aug. 20, 1835; proved Nov. 25, 1835. Children, Ann Sharp, John H. and Rachel. Son-in-law, Joseph Sharp.

WOODRUFF

Anna, Bridgeton, will July 26, 1852; proved Aug. 28, 1852. Daughter, Ruth.

David, Hopewell, will Nov. 6, 1818; proved July 9, 1822. Wife, Eunice. Children, Amy Veal, Israel, Phebe, Uriah D., Noah (dec'd), and David. Grandchildren, Mary, Anna and David, children of Noah Woodruff.

David, Bridgeton, will July 27, 1854; proved July 31, 1856. Wife, Matilda. Mother, Nancy Rocap.

Ebenezer, Deerfield, will Aug. 4, 1755; proved Sept. 13, 1755. Wife, Meriam. Children, Isaac, Ebenezer, Mary, Phebe, Rachel, Meriam and Hannah.

Enos, Greenwich, will Nov. 16, 1794; proved June 21, 1796. Wife mentioned, but not by name. Children, Abner, Enos, Mary Sayre, Sarah Maskell and Sabra Peck.

John, Hopewell, will May 1, 1755; proved May 23, 1755. Wife, Lidia. Children, John, Jesse, Benjamin, Ester, Lidia, James, David, Timothy and Catura.

John, Hopewell, will Aug. 13, 1793; proved Apr. 15, 1794. Wife, Phebe. Children, John, Stratton, Silas, Benjamin, Ephraim, Kiturah Carns and William.

John, Deerfield, will Dec. 20, 1813; proved Dec. 12, 1816. Wife, Susanna. Children, Johathan, Ephraim, William, Enos, Daniel and Ruth Carll.

John, Bridgeton, will Feb. 8, 1889; proved Mar. 6, 1839. Wife, Ruth. Grandson, John W. Applegate.

Lovice, Bridgeton, will Oct. 9, 1818; proved Dec. 26, 1820. Children, Jesse, Daniel, Jared and Thomas. Daughter-in-law, Ruth, wife of Daniel, and Elizabeth, wife of Thomas. Granddaughters, Lovice Parvin, daughter of Daniel and Ruth Woodruff, and Sarah, daughter of Jared Woodruff.

Sarah, Greenwich, will Jan. 31, 1797; proved Feb. 20, 1799. Children, Mary Sayre, Sarah Maskell and Sabra Peck. Grandchildren, Enos, son of Abner Woodruff, and Elizabeth.

Sarah, Fairfield, will Sept. 16, 1834; proved Sept. 29, 1837. Grandson, Henry G. Ogden.

Zebulon, Fairfield, will June 27, 1808; proved Mar. 20, 1813. Wife, Mary. Children, Josiah and Lydia. Cousins, Phebe and Israel, children of Phebe Woodruff.

WRIGHT

David, will Feb. 18, 1837; proved May 31, 1859. Wife, Mary. Brother, William Wright. Wife's daughter, Mary Ann Tillson.

William, Stoe Creek, will Apr. 4, 1827; proved July 19, 1828. Children, Hezekiah, Amon, William and Jane G.

WYNN

Isaac, Millville, will Feb. 3, 1846; proved Nov. 16, 1849. Children, Rebecca I., William P. and Benjamin I. Sister, Elizabeth Wynn.

YOUNG

Willinm, Downe, will May 5, 1797; proved Mar. 29, 1798. Wife, Sarah. Children, Ruth, James, Joseph and William. Brother, Joseph Young.

YOUNGS

Brown, Hopewell, will Aug. 3, 1797; proved Sept. 25, 1797. Wife, Martha. Children mentioned, but not by name.

Jonathan, Hopewell, will Mar. 7, 1790; proved 1791. Wife, Esther. Children, Lewis, Jonathan, Jeremiah, Samuel, Hannah, Lucy and Phebe. Brother, Brown Youngs.

INDEX

Persons whose Surnames are Different from that of the Testators

Ackley, Abigail, 17.
Acton, Benjamin, 40; Hannah, 40.
Alderman, Abigail, 66; Sarah, 44.
Allen, Delilah, 48; Kent, 48.
Anderson, Sarah, 105.
Andrews, Hannah, 48; Samuel, 48.
Applegate, John W., 137; Ruth, 130.
Appleton, Susan, 20.
Armstrong, Georg, 32.
Asstins, Priscilla, 13.
Avery, Jemima, 78; John L., 78.
Avis Christianna, 122; Mary Ann, 122.
Ayars, Abigail, 88; Amasa, 41; Enoch, 41; Hannah, 10; Jane, 114; Jonathan S., 36; Joseph, 46; Keziah, 46; Lydia, 115; Naomi, 110; Sarah, 41.
Ayers, Rachel, 48; Susannah, 73.
Ayres, Ann, 125; Anne, 41; Ephraim P., 57; Hannah, 10; Jonathan, 36; Lewis, 48; Nathan D., 10; Phebe, 126; Sarah, 36, 57; Zilla, 19.
Bacon, Adaline J., 102; Amos, 43; Barbara, 69; Charles, 40, 42; Daniel, 43; David, 98, 129; Delzel, 20; Eliza Ann, 136; Elizabeth, 66; Enos E., 49; Ephraim, 19, 49; George, 136; Isaac, 98; James, 98; Jemima, 124; Job, 136; Joseph, 43; Luce, 43; Mary, 20, 43; Rachel, 113; Rebecca M., 7, 20; Samuel, 65; Sarah, 20, 53, 89, 115; Sarah F., 49; Thomas, 42; William, 20
Baker, Benjamin, 69; Christopher, 69.
Baner, Sarah, 75.
Banks, Mary, 94.

Barracliff, Mary, 90.
Barratt, Caleb, 6; Moses. 14; William, 6; Zurviah, 46.
Barton, Rhoda, 92.
Bateman, Aaron, 86; Abigail, 50; Benjamin, 47; Charles, 47; Elizabeth, 86; Esther, 47; Hannah, 111; Harvey, 44; Jane E., 44; Lovina. 117; Thomas, 93; Victorina, 5, 22; William, 47.
Bates, Hannah, 124; John J., 124.
Beidman, Jacob, 76; Mary Jane, 76.
Bennet, Dorcas, 13; Elijah, 75; Elizabeth, 13; Isaac, 13; James, 13, 75; Lois, 44; Mary, 102; Rachel, 15, 75; Rebecca, 17; Samuel, 102.
Bennett, Hannah. 136; Leonard, 136.
Benson, Harriet, 40; Samuel, 40.
Bentley, Hannah, 107.
Berreen, Abigail, 134.
Bickley, Caroline, 23; Horace. 23.
Biddle, Elizabeth, 56; William, 56.
Bidwell, George, 40; Phebe 40.
Bigs, Mary, 34.
Biggs, Aaron, 103; Abigail, 102, 103; .Benjamin, 17; Elizabeth, 17; Ephraim, 103; Hannah, 20; Lazer, 103; Nehemiah, 103; Noah, 103; Thomas, 20; William, 103.
Bishop, Anna, 134; Eunice, 104; Mary, 93, 102.
Bivins, Joseph, 7; Sarah, 7; Thomas, 7.
Black, Phebe, 56.
Blackman, Hannah S., 65; John, 106; Ruth, 106.
Blackson, Louisa, 53.
Blew, Abijah, 83; Elanner, 83; Elizabeth, 83; Hannah, 87; George, 83; Seeley, 83.
Blizard, Elizabeth, 84; Naomi, 14; Rebeka, 14.
Blizzard, Elizabeth P., 128; Mary, 20.
Bluy, Harriet, 5.
Bond, Harriet, 134; Susanna, 42.
Bonham, Pacience, 6; Susan B., 7.
Borden, Abigail, 124.
Borton, Jacomintia, 50.
Bowen, Alvira, 124; Ananias. 74; David, 112; Deborah, 35; Eleanor, 33; Elizabeth, 35, 66, 124; Grace, 43; James, 96; Jonathan, 90; Lucy, 112; Mara, 90; Margaret, 121; Mary, 35, 38; Miriam, 76;

Phebe, 74, 96; Ruth, 67; Sarah, 35, 122; Susan Jane, 40; Thomas, 40.

Bowers, Deborah, 125; Ebenezer, 112; John, 101; Mary, 35; Naomi, 35; Ruth, 67; Susanna, 112.

Boyd, Amey, 63.

Brandriff, Caroline, 124; Isaac, 124.

Brewster, Ann, 132; Eunice, 18; Jackson, 18; Maria, 132; Rebecca, 129.

Brick, Mary, 21.

Bright, Elizabeth, 45; William, 45.

Brooks. Abigail, 67, 116; Alpheus, 66; Barsheba, 67; Burrhus, 21; Dolley, 48; Dorothy, 113; Isaac, 67; Jecomintie, 48; Keturah, 59; Lucy, 21; Martha, 113; Mary, 36, 39; Rachel B., 40; Rachel S., 59; Ruth, 67.

Brown, Elizabeth, 82, 91; Isaac, 81; Jacob, 23; Mary, 86.

Brual, Mary, 136,

Buck, Ephraim, 109; Jane, 21; Jeremiah, 18; John, 21; Sarah, 18.

Budd, Abigail, 60.

Burch, Abigail, 77; Daniel Elmer 77; Hester, 41.

Burk, Rhoda, 72.

Burrows, Priscilla, 21.

Burt, Anna, 68; Lodemy, 13.

Burton, Ann, 133; Henry, 133.

Busby, Mary, 32; Rhoda, 60.

Bush, Jane, 39; Tabitha, 89.

Butcher, Harriet, 46.

Buzby, Daniel, 46; Mary, 46.

Cake, Abigail, 41; James, 37; Julian, 37; Mary, 37, 78; Nancy, 37; Phebe, 88.

Caldwell, Hannah, 76.

Callahan, Susannah, 96.

Camm, Damaris, 92.

Campbell, Archibald, 78; Joseph, 17; Philey, 17.

Carl, Phebe, 80; Rachel, 87.

Carlisle, Priscilla, 68.

Carll, Damaris, 92; David, 121; Esther P., 39; Lydia, 92; Ruth, 137.

Carnes, David, 105; Ephraim, 105; Kiturah, 137; Mary, 105.

Carr, Elizabeth, 71; Rebecca, 71.

Caruthers, George, 37; Obadiah, 107; Philena, 87; Richard, 106; Samuel, 107.

Castow, Ami, 103
Causon, John, 60.
Cerbe, Stephen, 97.
Chambers, Elizabeth, 30; Hannah, 30; Mary, 30.
Chamlis, Christian, 56; Joseph, 56.
Chard, Benjamin, 63.
Chase, Sarah, 26.
Cheasmond, David, 114.
Cheesman, Abel G., 62; George P., 62.
Christian, Elizabeth, 89.
Chroell, Rachel, 100.
Clark, Anna, 18; Daniel, 18; Jeremiah, 35; Joel, 18; John, 103; Mary, 18; Phebe, 18; Rachel, 23, 53; Sarah, 35, 67; Stephen G. 132; Susannah, 27.
Claypoole, Hannah, 31; Harriet B., 130; Jesse D., 130.
Clements, Aaron, 10; Jane, 10; Phebe Ann, 132; Jebedee, 132.
Clever, Hannah O., 66.
Clothier, Anna, 75; William, 75.
Clunn, Francis Elmer, 85.
Cobb, John, 122; Kesiah, 122; Sarah, 99.
Coffin, Mary, 90.
Coles, Sarah, 115.
Colvin, Ruth, 53.
Collwell, Elijah, 15; Sarah, 15.
Compton, Aden, 46; Beulah, 28; Elizabeth, 46, 81; Hannah, 28, 29; Lucy, 80; Mary, 28, 46; Samuel, 80.
Conklin, Sarah, 111.
Connor, Lydia, 115; William, 115.
Conover, Barbara, 106.
Conrow, Tabitha, 84.
Cook, Abigail, 66; Jonathan, 66.
Coombs, Ann Maria, 81; Jane, 122; John, 122; Lydia Ann, 122; Susannah, 64.
Corey, John, 16; Lydia, 16.
Corson, Flowrander, 80; Isaac, 34; Isabella, 76.
Covoing, Mary, 57.
Cox, Rochel, 125.
Couch, Rachel, 20, 90.
Cotlter, Mary, 107.

Craig, Lydia, 34.
Crandol, Charity, 70; Claricy, 116.
Cronenberger, Catharine, 69.
Crossley, Mary, 128.
Cullen, Rebecca, 78.
Cummins, Lydia, 20.
Current, Mary, 71.
Daniels, Susan, 112; Thomas, 43.
Dare, Ann, 129; Benjamin, 89, 112, 113; David, 51; Edmond, 129; Elenor, 59; Elizabeth, 122; Elizabeth S., 53; Joseph, 95; Levi, 41; Mary, 18, 115; Millisent, 89; Mulford, 89; Phebe, 113; Polly, 128; Priscilla, 95; Rachel, 115; Rebecka, 122; Rinear, 51; Samuel, 89.
Darman, Sarah, 81.
Darvin, Ebenezer, 108.
Daten Elizabeth, 16; Lucy, 62; Peter, 62.
Daton, Ephraim, 41; Freelove, 41; Joseph, 41; Ruth, 26;
Daughty, Hannah, 83.
Davis, Abel, 8; Abigail, 73; Belford E., 8; David, 114; Ebenezer, 127; Edmund, 114; Elizabeth, 7; Esther, 103; Hannah, 114; Isaac N., 10; Phebe, 114; Reuben, 114; Rhoda, 98; Richard B., 8; Robert Dayton, 10; Sarah, 46, 86; Tamar, 8; Theophilus, 115.
Dayton Ephraim, 47; Ruhameleo, 47.
Dean, Keziah, 14.
Denn, Davis, 43.
Dennis, Charles, Jr., 50.
Denny, Esther, 122.
Diament, Mary, 49; Nathaniel, 98; Rhoda, 44; Susan, 65.
Dickson, Hannah, 119; Elener, 12.
Doilas, Ann, 54; Elizabeth, 32, 54; Ruth, 106; William, 80.
Dollass, Elizabeth, 18; Jonathan, 18.
Dorton, Elizabeth, 16; John, 14.
Doughty, Joseph, 62; Prudence, 62.
Douglas, Abigail, 76.
Downam, Ellen, 115; Richard, 115.
Drummond, Silvia, 84.
DuBois, Benjamin, 107; Jeremiah, 117; Mary, 107; Sarah, 53.
Duffee, Elizabeth, 70.
Duffee, Marthew; 135.
Duffel, Hannah, 136.

Dun, Elizabeth, 133.
Dunham, Amey, 46; Ann, 57; David, 115; Polly, 115.
Dunlap, Charity, 119; Elizabeth, 23.
Dunn, Benjamin, 40; Edith, 40; Peggy, 27.
Dunnum, Elizabeth, 128.
Duvall, Eunice, 74; Joel, 74.
Edmunds, Ann M., 83; Franklin D., 83.
Edwards, Annanias, 121; Ruth, 73; Sarah, 33, 127; Susanna, 121.
Eldreg, Hannah, 54.
Eldridge, Mary, 8.
Elmer, Abigail, 37; Benjamin, 132; Daniel, 77, 82; Horace, 82; Jonathan, 102, 111; Margaret, 100; Martha, 94; Mary, 111; Nancy, 101; Rachel, 5; Rumolla, 5; Ruth S., 15; Timothy, 15.
Elwell, David, 74; Hannah, 116; Isaac, 84; Lovisa, 80; Rachel 116; Samuel,, 116; William, 74.
Endicot, Berzila, 114; Elizabeth, 114.
Errickson, Fannie, 70; Hollingshead, 70; Raechl, 35; Sarah, 60; Silsby, 35.
Evans, Ann, 46; David, 46; Edward, 46; George, 46; Hannah, 135; Jacob, 100; Jean, 100, Mary, 100; Sarah, 119.
Ewing, Deliverance, 122; Hannah, 66; James I., 64; James Josiah, 111; John, 9; Martha, 64; Mary, 95; Remington, 105; Sarah, 30; William, 105.
Falkner, Eleanor, 25.
Fight, Sarah 15.
Fithian, Charles, 49; Charles B., 49; Deborah, 47; Enoch, 21; Enos E., 49; Erkuries, 64; Hannah, 64; Hope, 107; Humphrey, 33; Isaac, 130; Joel, 23; John, 27; Jonathan, Jr., 112; Joseph, 44; Josiah, 18; Lodemy, 13; Lot, 92; Lovisa, 92; Mary, 49; Matilda, 99; Phebe, 33; Rachel, 18, 78; Rhoda, 100; Ruth, 23, 44; Sarah, 54, 88, 92; Samuel, 74; Seeley, 27.
Forbes, Catharine, 104.
Forsman, Mary, 76.
Foster, Cintha, 102; Christopher, 56; Elizabeth, 56; Hannah, 99, 120; Isaac P., 44; Mary, 135; Nathaniel, 120; Preston, 44; Rosina, 44.
Fouller, Hugh, 70.
Fowler, William, 70,
Fox, Catharine, 61; Elizabeth, 121; George, 61; William, 117.

Francis, Tabitha, 7.
Frazer, David, 41.
Frazeur, Sarah, 41.
Frazier, John, 39
Frazure, Mary, 92; Rebecca, 39.
Frederick, John, 79; Lovisa, 79.
Freeland, Lydda, 128.
Freeman, Margaret, 75; Mary, 103.
Freese, Catharine, 74.
French, Elizabeth, 98.
Fuller, Martha, 92.
Gagers, Hannah, 57.
Ganon, Abia, 99.
Gardner, Hope, 106; James, 107.
Garrison, Arthur, 34; Edith, 82; Edmund, 78; Elenor, 119; Eliza, 92; Elizabeth, 34, 120; Hannah, 34; John, 124; Lydia, 104; Maria, 89; Mary, 78, 84, 93; Powell, 124; Rebecca, 37; Ruth, 38, 94; Sary, 61; Statia, 124; Stephen, 34.
Garten, Anne, 91.
Garton, Athelah, 109; Catharine, 121; Daniel, 109; Elizabeth, 121; Gabriel, 109; Hosea, 121; Jonathan, 121; Margaret, 16; Mary, 121.
Gentry, Hannah, 14.
Gibbon, Esther, 111; John, 111.
Giles, Fannie Holmes, 18; Hannah, 18; James, 18; Mary Bloomfield, 18.
Gilman, Isaac Fithian, 52; Mary, 104; Lydia, 79; Rebecca, 65; Rebecca, 65; Uriah, 104; William, 52.
Githens, Elvira J., 32; Mary D., 32; W. Lewis, 32.
Glaspey, Ephraim S., 115; Hannah B., 115; Rachel, 53.
Glassby, Rachel, 57.
Goff, Caroline, 92; **Martha**, 92.
Golder, Bethina, 35; Jacob, 35.
Goodrat, Bershabe, 55.
Gould, Susy, 98.
Green, Hannah, 76.
Griggery, Elizabeth, 76.
Gruff. Elizabeth, 126.
Haas, Calvin, 66; Edwin, 66; Phebe M., 66.
Haines, Rachel, 51.

Haley, David, 111; Hannah, 111; Ruth, 68.

Hall, Aaron, 7; Abel, 40; Caleb, 7; Ebenezer, 40; Ebenezer M., 42; Elizabeth, 25, 136; Esther, 19; Hannah, 12; Hannah L, 66; Joseph, 111; Levi, 19; Levi B., 7; Mark, 40; Mary, 23; Moses, 42; Prudence, 36; Sarah, 40, 115.

Hampton, Fannie, 59; Isaac H., 132; Isaac W., 59.

Hancock, Hannah, 23.

Hand, Judith, 13; Margaret, 20.

Hankins, Elizabeth, 127; Elmer, 96; Lydia, 96.

Hann, Serenah, 119.

Hanna, Dolly, 35.

Hannah, Bathsheba, 89; Hannah Ann, 119; Martha, 89.

Hannon, Joseph, 86; Mary, 92; Joseph, 42.

Harmer, Sarah, 31.

Harris, Abigail, 27, 86, 95, 124; Adeline, 132; Alva, 10; Amy, 115; Ann, 121; David, 27, 44; Elizabeth, 10; Enos, 39; Ephraim, 42, 100; Hannah, 42; Isaac W., 132; Jacob, 35; James, 121; James W., 135; Jane, 86, 91; Jeremiah, 86; John, 9; Judith, 92; Lydia, 39; Pierson, 92; Rachel, 5; Rebecca, 40; Ruth, 94; Sarah, 126; Thomas, 93; 108; Tirza, 126; Violetta, 37.

Harrow, Maria, 115.

Hasen, Emeline, 12, Emily, 12.

Hays, Abigail, 108.

Heaton, David, 76; Ruth, 60; Sarah, 75.

Helton, Jerusha, 19; Sarah, 19.

Henderson, Jerusha, 92; John, 44; Theodosia, 44.

Hepner, Mary, 69.

Heritage, Ann, 123; Jacob, 124; Job, 124; Lemuel, 114.

Hess, Elmer, 69; George, 69.

Heward, Esther, 94.

Hewet, Elener, 17; Elishabe, 55; Mary, 55.

Hewitt, Elizabeth R., 84; Genet, 62; Noah, 84.

Hews, Meribe, 28.

Hickman, Hester, 17; Joseph, 17.

Higbee, Theodore, 34.

Higby, Mary, 34; Theodore B., 34.

High, Mary, 20, 41; Samuel D., 41.

Hildridge, Elizabeth, 14.

Hinchman, Miriam, 103.

Hitchner, Adam, 64; Matthias, 64; Sarah, 64.
Hoffman, Elizabeth, 30; Jemimah, 78; Jonathan, 30.
Hogben, Lucy, 20.
Holland, Sylvia, 122.
Hollingshead, Hannah, 61; Samuel, 61.
Holmes, Abijah, 18, 31, 111; Anna, 18; Ephraim, 18; John, 18; Jonathan, 18; Rachel, 111.
Hood, Daniel Elmer, 25; Elizabeth, 7; Phebe, 25; Robert, 7;.
Hoover, Catherine, 30; Elizabeth, 56; Ellen, 76; George, 76; Jacob, 30; Peter, 30; Samuel, 30.
Horton, Hannah, 122.
Hosiel, Elizabeth, 70; George, 70; Henry, 70; Mary, 70.
Houseman, Amy, 101; Sarah, 136.
Howell, Abigail, 44; Caroline, 96; Charles, 44, 99; Hannah, 93; Margaret, 132; Nathaniel, 14.
Hudson, Rachel, 133.
Huffman, Dorty, 70; Polly, 70.
Huggins, Sarah, 126.
Hughes, Aaron, 29.
Huings, Sarah, 49.
Huit, Elishaba, 55.
Hunter, Unice, 30
Husted, Daniel, 25; David, 9; Harriet, 104; John, 89; Jonathan, 89; Phebe, 89; Ruth, 132. Sarah, 8, 25, 119.
Hutton, Angelina, 53; James, 53; Mary Ann, 53.
Ingersoll, Roxanna, 60
Ingersull, Drusilla, 69.
Inskeep, Abraham, 18; Abraham H., 59; Maria, 59.
Irelan, Hannah, 115; Sarah, 16.
Ireland, Charles G., 56; Daniel, 56; Esther, 41; Lydia, 56; Mary, 41.
Isley, Sarah, 96.
Jackson, Ann, 33; Jethro, 33.
James, Elizabeth, 35; Helen, 13; Patience, 53.
Jameson, Rachel, 93.
Jarl, Hannah H., 45.
Jarman, Jonathan, 12; Reuben, 12.
Jeffers, Ruth 132.
Jeffrys, Rebecca, 28.

Jenkins, Dorcas, 134; Mary, 24; Samuel, 134.

Jerrel, Bower, 45.

Jessop, Mary, 38.

Johnson, Annabel, 15; Hannah, 29; Jacob, 26; Josiah, 86; Latitia, 86; Macklenah, 106; Mary, 48; Othnial, 48; Perry, 127; Prudence 116; Rhoda, 37.

Johnston, Elizabeth, 71, 104; George, 19; Margaret, 71; Mary, 19; Sally, 110.

Jones, Abial, 19; Ann, 136; Hannah, 93; Meriah Ogden, 58; Priscilla, 122; Sarah, 19; Zipporah, 77.

Joslin, Phebe, 34.

Josling, Christian, 57.

Kane, Mehitable, 127.

Katts, John, 69; Margaret, 68, 69.

Keen, Benjamin, 61; Lodemah, 60.

Kelsay, Hannah, 116; Harriet, 115; Joseph, 76; Josiah, 115; Robert, 76.

Kenamon, Cecelia, 23.

Kimsey, Betsey, 31; Charlotte, 31; Rebecca, 31.

King, Ellen C., 107.

Kinley, Sarah, 59.

Ladow, Ruth, 128; Rusel, 103.

Lafferty, Dorothy, 104; Eliza, 104; Jane, 104.

Lake, Unice, 57.

Lane, Ann F., 126.

Laning, John, 132.

Lasley, Mary, 55; Thomas, 55.

Lathbury, Phebe, 84.

Laurence, Jonathan, 93; Mary, 112; Rachel, 91.

Lawrence, Anna, 95; Franklin, 132; Hannah, 93; Harriet, 80; Jonathan, 112; Ruth, 67; Zepporah, 120.

Leake, Hannah, 23, 53, 58; Levi, 57; Mable, 104; Mary, 57; Ruth, 58.

Lee, Charles W., 92; Deborah W., 92; Edwin F., 92; Hugh H., 92; Lydia, 92; Mary, 122; Naomi, 92; Sarah C., 107; Thomas, 92; Thomas F., 92.

Leslie, Lovise, 86.

Lester, Catharine, 123.

Lock, Juda, 128; Margit, 128.

Long, Claudius, 134; David, 36; Margaret, 50; Rebecca, 134.
Loper, Daniel, 58; Mary, 21; Rachel, 20; Ruth, 129; Sarah, 58.
Lorance, Jonathan, 37; Nathan, 37.
Lore. Ann, 54; Dollas, 45; Ephraim, 54; Hannah, 60; Hezekiah, 45; James, 126; John, 55, 115; Jonathan, 54, 60, 62; Nancy, 33; Nathaniel, 54; Phebe, 54; Rebecca, 60; Reuben, 111; Rhoda, 115; Sarah, 46; Seth, 54; Thomas Jefferson, 126; Uriah, 60; William, 54.
Low, Mary, 70.
Lowery, Ann Maria, 14; Elizabeth, 14; John T., 14; Mary G., 14. Sarah T., 14.
Ludlam, Norton, 11; Phebe, 11; Providence, 113, 130, 132.
Lummis, Almeda, 77; Charlotte, 96; Elizabeth, 77; Elizabeth W., 135; Hannah, 26; Hannah D., 135; Hetty, 94; John O., 94; Lydia, 94; Margaret, 121; Martha, 94; Mary, 77; Nancy, 94; Rachel, 93, 94 Rufus R., 77.
Lupton, Cynthia, 66; Lydia, 66; Mary, 16.
Machesney, William, 88.
Marlin, Margaret, 56.
Marshall, Jane Ann, 104; Mary, 104.
Maskell, Abijah, 52; Enoch, 52; John W., 135; Sally, 52; Sarah, 130, 137; Silvester, 52; Thomas A., 135.
Mason, David, 62; Phebe, 62.
Matthews, Bethia, 87; Ludlam, 125; Mary, 102; Rachel, 125; Temperance, 21.
Mattson, Emily, 94; Matilda, 94; Rachel, 93.
Maul, Ashbury, 84; Benjamin, 52; Benjamin F., 10; B. Franklin, 10; Elizabeth, 52; Phebe, 90; Rachel, 57; Sarah, 10.
Mayhew, Ann, 60; Catharine, 60; Esther, 94.
McCarty, Elizabeth, 76.
McChesney, Hannah, 97.
McClong, Agnes, 19.
McCormack, John, 123; Nancy, 123.
McCollen, Sarah, 56; Thomas, 56.
McElroy, Elizabeth, 98.
McFerson, James, 6; Rachel, 88.
McGilliard, Ann, 61; Hannah, 104.
McGrange, Hannah, 14; John, 14; William, 14.
McIlvaine, Maria, 18.
McLain, Elizabeth, 21; Hannah, 21; Robert, 21.

McLong, Rebecca, 87.
McMungall, Esther, 19.
McPherson, Azariah, 88; Elizabeth, 84.
McQueen, Hannah, 53, 120.
McWilliams, Hannah Ann, 84; William, 84.
Mead, Rebecca, 92.
Medcalf, Elizabeth, 115.

Miller, Abigail. 104; Ann, 116; Charles, 53; Elizabeth, 89, 130; Experience, 103; George, 122; Hannah, 89; Harriet N., 53; John, 103; Joseph, 78; Patience, 39; Rachel, 42, 103; Richard, 71; Sally, 71; Sarah W., 130; Stephen, 27; William, 43.

Mills, Daniel, 95; David, 95; Dorcas, 122.
Minch, David, 36; Precilla, 90; Sarah, 36.
Moncrief, Rachel, 84.

Moore, Amy, 23, 53; Bowen, 107; Daniel, 76; Elijah, 19; Hannah, 106, 107, 114; James, 76; Jane, 132; Joel 111; John, 107; John P., 132; Keziah, 76; Mary P., 101; Orpha, 91; Phebe, 21; Priscilla, 110, 115; Ruhamey, 19; Ruth, 39; Sarah, 76. 104.

Morrison, Judah, 33; Nathan, 119; William, 33.
Morrow, David R., 40.
Moslander, Grace, 70.

Mulford, Elizabeth, 12; Emma D., 51; Enoch, 52; Frances, 37; Hannah, 59; Jacob, 51; Jane, 51; Mary Ann, 51, 53; Phebe, 66; Rhoda, 77; Samuel, 59; Sarah, 119; Thomas, 106.

Murphew, James, 19; Prudence, 19.
Murphey, Daniel, 40; Susannah, 40.
Murphy, Betsey, 128; Prudence, 28; Susannah, 55.
Murry, Angelina, 99; Uthniel, 99.
Nealy, Elizabeth, 19; John, 19; Joseph, 19.
Neidy, Edith, 55.
Neill, Sarah, 47, William, Rev. Dr., 47.
Newbold, Deborah, 43; Samuel, 43.

Newcomb, David, 115; Elizabeth, 13; Ephraim, 101; Hannah, 44; Isaac, 44; John P., 128; John R., 128; Joseph, 116; Martha S., 116; Naomi, 103; Phebe, 100; Pleasant, 79; Polly, 13; William, 79.

Newkirk, Caroline, 109; Elizabeth, 53; John, 109, Lovina, 109; Oliver, 109; Ruth, 109.

Nichols, Bathsheba, 107; James, 40; Rebecca, 40; Walter, 107.
Nickles, Rode, 111.

FROM CUMBERLAND COUNTY WILLS

Nickol, Mary, 19.
Nieukirk, Ann, 107.
Nixon, Ruth, 124.
Noble, Daniel, 67; Elizabeth, 10; Margaret, 67.
Nottingham, Mary Ann, 125.
Ogden, Abigail, 23; Bathniphleath, 26; Elmer, 47; Hannah, 38; Harriet, 82; Henry G., 137; Jason, 47; Jedidiah, 97; Martha; 83, Mary, 47; Mary B., 127; Sarah, 57, 67, 109; Temperance, 53; Theodosia T., 127; Thomas Harris, 127.
Orr, Sarah, 128; Unis, 76.
Osler, Benjamin, 123; Eliza, 123; Kitturah, 123; Mary, 123; Priscilla, 123.
Osterhout, Elizabeth, 78.
Ott, Christiana, 64.
Padget, Amy, 83; Gamaliel, 74; Sarah, 122.
Page, Grace, 91, 115; John, 31; Mary, 103; Ruth, 92.
Paris, Mary, 56.
Parsons, James, 11; Phebe, 20.
Parvin, Anna M., 105; Azuba, 37; Benjamin, 22; David, 82; Hannah, 6; Lovisa, 82; Rachel, 66, 82; Sarah, 105, 124; Susannah, 117; Uriah, 66.
Pasley, Elizabeth, 60.
Paul, Almarine 25; Hiram, 24; Phebe, 24, 25; Sarah, 25.
Paulin, Elizabeth, 135; Margaret, 135; Phebe, 116; Rebecca, 39; William 113.
Pearson, Mary, 134.
Peck, Jane, 42; Rebecca, 23; Sabra, 84, 137; Thomas, 42.
Penton, Elizabeth, 31.
Perrey, Anay, 21.
Perry, Jeremiah, 41; Sarah, 41.
Peterson, Abyah, 102; Catharin, 102; Christiana, 49; Dare, 125; Deborah, 39; Dorcas, 44; Elizabeth, 74; Hannah, 125; Mary, 69; Polly, 90; Purple, 102; Sarah, 30, 125.
Pew, Mary, 33.
Pierson, Azel, 18; Daniel, 131; Elizabeth, 102; Martha, 63; Nancy, 94; Phebe, 18.
Pine, Emma, 119; Mary Jane, 119; Priscilla, 119; Rachel S., 119.
Platts, Letitia, 87; Nancy, 87; Rachel, 57; Thomas, 28.
Plummer, Elizabeth, 119.

Poor, Hannah, 108; Solomon, 108.
Porch, Ruth, 58; William, 58.
Porter, Edward M., 119; Harriet, 89.
Potter, Hannah, 16, 22; Henry, 16; James B., 22; Robert B., 22.
Powell, Charlotte, 119; Elizabeth, 72; Henry, 14, 55; John, 55; Rebecca, 14; Rhoda, 134; Richard, 72; Ruth, 44; Theodosia, 92.
Preston, Elizabeth, 38; Hannah, 21; Miriam, 56,
Prickett, Mary, 28.
Probasco, John, 11; Lydia Ann W., 130; Mary, 11; Priscilla, 130; Richard L., 130.
Quixel, Ruth, 17.
Rammel, Catharina, 69; Christiana, 69.
Ramsay, Ephraim, 111, 120; James, 111; John, 120; Nancy, 120; Rebecca, 120; Sarah, 111.
Randall, Abigail, 20; David, 20.
Randolph, David, 90; Elizabeth, 8; Isaac S. F., 7; Jacob, 6; Jane Eliza, 7; Lewis, 114; Margaret, 6; Margaret F., 39, 114; Martha, 114; Sally, 7.
Rankin, Rachel, 9.
Ranny, Stephen, 129.
Ranshart, Christiana, 70.
Ray, Abigail, 12, 47, 48; James, 12, 47, 48; Mary, 89; Susannah, 82.
Read, Charles, 59; Nancy, 59,
Reed, Rachel, 21; Sarah, 133.
Reeve, Elizabeth, 23, 41; Martha, 9; Rachel, 128.
Reeves, Cynthia, 42; Hannah, 94; Jacob, 116; John, 74; Johnson, 74; Lemuel, 74; Mabel, 74; Phebe, 112; Priscilla W., 115; Rachel, 42, 60; Sarah, 73; William, 94.
Regain, Anne, 70.
Reminton, Moses, 113; Rachel, 113.
Remington, Sarah, 81; Theodosha, 109.
Reves, John, 31; Katherine, 20; Sarah, 57.
Richardson, Jeremiah, 111; Joseph, 111; Robert, 95; William, 122.
Richer, Ananias G., 110; Jacob, 110; Maria, 110.
Richerson, John, 43; Richard, 43; Robert, 43; William, 43.
Riel, Mary, 46.
Riley, Eleanor, 92; James M., 34; Ruth, 34, 97.
Robbins, David, 29; Elizabeth, 29; Mary, 14; Obadiah, 9, 70;

Robbins, Rachel, 9, 10; Rebecca, 5; Sarah, 87.

Roberts, Mary, 19, 20.

Robertson, Christiana, 62; Hosea, 114; Prudence, 114.

Robeson, Mary, 106; Robbins, 106; Web, 106

Robins, Abigail, 6.

Robinson, Abraham, 19; Amariah, 11; Ann Elizabeth, 92; Dan, 14; Eli, 19; Elkanah, 30; Elizabeth, 21, 113, 119; Ellis, 19; Esther H., 92; Hosea, 19; Jonn, 30; Letisha C., 59; Nancy, 11; Rebecka, 19; Sarah, 13, 30; Steelman, 30.

Rocap, Nancy, 136; Salome, 69.

Rogers, Hannah, 85.

Rose, Catharine, 110; John, 11; Phebe, 53; Rachel, 11; Sally, 27

Royal, Hannah, 124,

Ross, Richard, 123; Thomas, 123.

Royall, David, 16, 29; Joel, 29; Mary, 16; Rachel, 29.

Rousman, Martha A. S., 111.

Rulon, Hannah, 43; John, 28; Nathaniel, 43.

Rulon, Sarah, 28.

Russe, Rebeckey, 76.

Russel, Charlotte, 28.

Rutter, Elizabeth, 90,

Sailer, Abigail, 56; William, 129; Zachariah, 129.

Sakel, Eve, 113,

Saxton, , Benjamin, 84; Sarah Ann, 84.

Sayre, Annanias, 103; Hannah, 122, 123; Kittary, 34; Mary, 9, 10, 137; Paciance, 87; Patience, 103; Rachel, 81, 114; Thomas, 79; William, 34.

Scott, Hannah, 88.

Seeley, Almeda, 66; David, 99; Ebenezer, 18, 83, 99; Eden M., 66.

Seward, Ellen L., 32; Ephraim, 102; Jesse, 72; Mary, 18, 72; Mary R., 83; Naomi, 99; Ruth, 99.

Sharp, Ann, 136; Catharine, 15; Delaney, 125; Joseph, 136; Lydia, 125; Mary, 33; Peter, 106; Sarah, 106.

Shaw, Elizabeth, 35, 93; Hannah, 116; Leonard, 12; Mary, 16; Nathan, 55; Sarah, 98.

Sheets, Sarah, 34.

Shepard, Abigail, 13, 39.

Shepherd, Amey, 20; Daniel, 9; Eleanor 79; Elizabeth, 37; John, 9; Jonadab, 24; Samuel, 14.

Sheppard, Abel, 12; Anna, 42; Anna M., 125; Annie, 39; Caleb, 39; Daniel, 106; Dicason, 41; Dickason, 41; Dickenson, 41; Dickeson, 42; Edith, 39; Ephraim, 119; Hannah, 41, 62, 73, 106; Harriet, 36; Henry, 78. James, 36; John, 56; Jonadab, 97; Margaret, 39, 42, 56; Mary M. 119; Melisa, 41; Phebe, 81; Priscilla H., 65; Rachel, 8, 106; Sarah, 136; Thomas, 59, 106; William T., 39.

Shimp, Catherine, 106.

Shinn, Abigail, 33; Allen, 33.

Shints, Joseph, 115; Ruth, 115.

Shoemaker, Charles, 65; Enoch, 65; Hannah, 89; Horace B., 65; James, 133; Sarah, 65.

Shropshire, Bennett, 35; Phebe, 35; Rebecca, 74.

Shull, Jonathan, 17; Matilda A., 40; Naomy, 38; Rachel, 17; Ruth D., 37; Susannah, 17; William, 40.

Shute, Eliza M., 87; Elizabeth, 111.

Simpkins, Hannah, 122.

Sickle Mary Magdalena, 69.

Smalley, Isaac M., 90.

Smith, Abigail, 94; Anna Maria, 65; Bathsheba, 40; Caty, 65; Charlotte, 65; Daniel, 40, 102; Edward, 84; Eleazar, 94; Elisha, 102; Elizabeth, 32, 44; Ephraim H., 65; Esther, 14, 84; Henrietta, 35; Isaac, 69; James, 60; Jane, 19, 82; Jemima, 57; Lovicy, 107; Lucy, 113; Maria, 69; Mary, 61; Mason, 19; Phebe, 110, Rebecca, 94; Rebecka, 19; Sarah, 60, 84, 94, 117, 133; Teresa, 81; William, 14.

Sneathen, Phebe, 53.

Snethen, Hosea, 117.

Sockwell, Martha, 20; Samuel, 20.

Souder, Elizabeth, 118; Philip, 118.

Sowder, Catharine, 95.

Stanger, Jane Ann, 78, 104.

Stanly, Catharine, 27.

Stathem, Susanna, 31.

Stedems, Priscilla, 93.

Steelman, Abel, 34; Hannah, 34.

Stevens, Amey, 119; Mary, 57.

Stevenson, Rachel, 128.

Stewart, Charles, 136.

Still, Ann, 60; Rachel, 56.

Stillwell, Jane, 74.

Stites, Benjamin, 31.
Stockton, Joseph, 19; Lydia, 88; Rachel, 19.
Stout, Rebecca, 123.
Stow, Francis, 122; Thomas, 122.
Stratton, Aaron, 110; Abigail, 67, 102; Caroline, 33; Deborah, 102; Esther, 53; Freelove, 102; Hannah, 39; Nancy, 19; Rebecca, 39; Sarah, 102; Thomasine, 102;
Streeper, Catharine, 24, 25; Christopher, 24; Clarence, 25.
Stretch, Daniel B., 44; Theodosia, 44.
Sutton, Letitia, 118; Ruth, 72.
Swain, Eleanor, 69; Jonathan, 69.
Sweatman, James, 102; Mary, 102; Rebecca, 102; Vartus, 102.
Swing, Polly, 50; Sarah, 44.
Swinney, Andrew J., 111; Anna S., 114; Claricy, 6; Ebenezer H., 111; Elisha, 20; Ephraim, 111; Kezia, 6; Vallantine, 6.
Synott, Martin, 38.
Tasker, Mene, 74.
Taylor, Elizabeth, 31; Ellen, 107; Jonathan, 31; Rhoda, 46.
Teril, Ephraim, 105.
Terry, Andrew, 38; Ephraim, 38; Hannah, 80; Jonah, 100; Jonah, 100; Josiah, 38; Patience, 38.
Thomas, Sarah, 41.
Thompson, Ann, D. C., 46; Anne Elmer, 77; Benjamin, 95; Deborah, 126; Elizabeth, 77; Martha, 115; Mary, 100; Matilda, 14; Moses, 78; Phebe, 57; Ruth, 53, 95; Samuel, 41.
Tice, Lydia, 117; Rachel, 117.
Tillson, Mary Ann, 138.
Tilsmires, Adam, 111.
Titas, Abigail 53.
Titsworth, Hannah Ann, 114.
Tomlin, Eliza, 125; Reuben, 125.
Tomlinson, Judith, 132; Lewis W., 66; Louisa, 16; Martha, 63; Nathan, 16; Thomas, 114.
Tomson, Hannah, 67.
Tribet, Sarah, 96; Thomas, 96.
Tribbitt, Sumner, 96; Susan Ann, 96.
Tucker, Naomi, 91.
Tuft, Mary, 18.
Tullis, Elena, 43; Mary, 67; Nancy, 81; William, 43.

156   GENEALOGICAL DATA

Tully, Mary, 80.
Tumbleson, Elizabeth, 31.
Tyler, Mary H., 111.
Vanaman, Elizabeth, 68.
Vanderford, Abraham, 17, 117; Caterena, 117; Mary, 17.
Vandusin, Abigail, 17.
VanHook, Mary, 55.
VanMeter, Caroline, 133; Edward, 133; Isaac, 121; Mary, 92; Sarah, 121.
Veal, Amy, 136.
Waddington, Elizabeth, 74.
Waithman, Clement, 36; John, 83; Thomas, 84.
Wainwright, Pamele, 69.
Ward, Elizabeth, 77; John, 123; Nancy, 132.
Ware, Ann, 101; Ahna, 9; Anne, 10; Elizabeth, 28; Harriet, 111; Mary, 98.
Warne, Mary L., 78; Ruth, 78.
Watson, Howell, 101; Isaac, 101, 129; John, 129; Phebe, 10; Sally, 81; Samuel, 10; William, 101.
Weathman, Constant, 106; Lydia, 106.
Webb, Elizabeth, 20.
Weeks, Mary, 106.
Welch, Edward, 67.
Weldon, Mary, 70; Rebecca D., 35.
Wells, Elizabeth, 46; James, 46.
West, Beulah, 102; Lucy, 42; Richard, 42.
Wescoat, Henry, 21; Rebeckah, 21.
Westcoat, Jehiel, 114; Joel, 93; Mary, 114; Rachel, 93.
Westcoate, Catharine, 80.
Westcot, Abigail, 54; Hannah, 54.
Westcott, Abigail, 93, 94; Damaris, 42; David, 19; Ephraim, 94; Harriet, 126; Harrison, 126; James, 42, 117; Jane, 65; John, 44; Mary, 19, 94, 119; Phebe, 96; Rachel, 38; Rebecca, 117; Robert, 94; Sarah, 38, 44, 91; William, 119.
Wheaton, Anna, 77; Judith, 81; Molly, 52.
Whitaker, Isaac, 78; Oliver, 78; Rachel, 21; Recompence, 78; William H., 116.
White, Claracy, 114; David, 101; Elizabeth, 59; Eparaim D., 101; Jane, 101; John E., 101; Mary, 64; Rebecca, 39; William, 64.

Whitecar, Abigail, 97; Rachel, 19.
Whiteman, Benjamin, 97; Mariah, 97.
Whitticar, Ruth, 66.
Wick, Edo, 6.
Wickward, Sarah, 32.
Wilkinson, Hannah, 53.
Willets, Hannah, 23; John Howard, 23.
Williams, James, 64; Mary, 22; Priscilla, 64.
Willock, Nancy, 71.
Wills, Aquilla, 46; Beulah, 46; Daniel, 46; David, 46; John, 46; Samuel, 46.
Wilmer, Hannah, 75.
Wilson, John, 125; Susan, 125.
Withers, George, 9; James, 9,
Wollan, Mary, 76.
Wood, Adnah, 6; Anne, 6, 75; Aulay, 128; Charles, 75; Charlotte, 109; David, 108; Elizabeth, 75; Ezra, 115; Hannah, 25, 75; Horatio, 75; Lewis, 39; Margaret, 19; Naomi, 39, 114; Obadiah, 6; Rachel, 128; Rebecca, 115; Richard, 75.
Woodrough, Sarah, 17.
Woodruff, Abner, 115; Ann, 74; Archibald, 36; Elizabeth, 37, 115; Enos, 75, 132; John, 75; Leonard, 111; Mary, 21; Phebe, 124; Rebecca, 36; Rhoda, 106; William, 75.
Woolson, Hance, 56; Rachel, 56.
Woolston, Martha, 96.
Worthington, Ephraim, 23; John, 23.
Wright, John, 58; Rachel, 58; Rhoda, 69.
Wynn, Benjamin, 111; Isaac, 102; Rebecca, 102, 103; Sarah, 111; Susan, 103, 111; William, 112.
Yapp, Lydia, 87.
Youngs, Naomi, 115; Sarah, 70.
Youstead, Priscilla Ann, 134.

www.ingramcontent.com/pod-product-compliance
Lightning Source LLC
Chambersburg PA
CBHW020653300426
44112CB00007B/370